NewRules@Work

NewRules@Work

**79 Etiquette Tips, Tools, and Techniques
to Get Ahead and Stay Ahead**

Barbara Pachter

with Ellen Schneid Coleman

PRENTICE HALL PRESS

PRENTICE HALL PRESS
Published by the Penguin Group
Penguin Group (USA) Inc.
375 Hudson Street, New York, New York 10014, USA
Penguin Group (Canada), 90 Eglinton Avenue East, Suite 700, Toronto, Ontario M4P 2Y3, Canada
(a division of Pearson Penguin Canada Inc.)
Penguin Books Ltd., 80 Strand, London WC2R 0RL, England
Penguin Group Ireland, 25 St. Stephen's Green, Dublin 2, Ireland (a division of Penguin Books Ltd.)
Penguin Group (Australia), 250 Camberwell Road, Camberwell, Victoria 3124, Australia
(a division of Pearson Australia Group Pty. Ltd.)
Penguin Books India Pvt. Ltd., 11 Community Centre, Panchsheel Park, New Delhi—110 017, India
Penguin Group (NZ), Cnr. Airborne and Rosedale Roads, Albany, Auckland 1310, New Zealand
(a division of Pearson New Zealand Ltd.)
Penguin Books (South Africa) (Pty.) Ltd., 24 Sturdee Avenue, Rosebank, Johannesburg 2196, South
Africa

Penguin Books Ltd., Registered Offices: 80 Strand, London WC2R 0RL, England

While the author has made every effort to provide accurate telephone numbers and Internet addresses at the time of publication, neither the publisher nor the author assumes any responsibility for errors, or for changes that occur after publication. Further, the publisher does not have any control over and does not assume any responsibility for author or third-party websites or their content.

First edition: September 2006

Library of Congress Cataloging-in-Publication Data

Pachter, Barbara.
    New rules @ work : 79 etiquette tips, tools, and techniques to get ahead and stay ahead / Barbara
Pachter ; with Ellen Schneid Coleman.
        p. cm.
    ISBN 978-0-7352-0407-2
    1. Business etiquette. 2. Business communication. I. Coleman, Ellen Schneid. II. Title.
III. Title: New Rules at work.
    HF5389.P3 2006
    395.5'2—dc22   2006019258

PRINTED IN THE UNITED STATES OF AMERICA

10 9 8 7 6 5

CONTENTS

INTRODUCTION

No Way! Who Would Do That?

Meet Jonathan. He graduated at the top of his class from an Ivy League school and then got his MBA from a leading business school. Jonathan quickly landed a high-level dream job as a technology consultant. Things were really going his way until his first client dinner. When he sat down at the table he put his chewing gum underneath his plate. Jonathan's new boss was appalled by his behavior; the client probably was, too, though he never said anything. The next day, in his boss's office, Jonathan was told, "If anything like that happens again, you're out of here."

You may say: "He didn't mean to do it. He probably didn't know. Cut him a break. It was an innocent mistake."

Or maybe you're saying, "No one would do that! I would never do that." And perhaps you wouldn't, but are you certain you wouldn't commit some other blunder—one with the potential to sideline your career?

People often believe you can slip up here and there and it won't matter in the long run. Take it from me: Your behavior, including the bloopers, blunders, and innocent mistakes matter. They can matter *big*-time!

I know this is true, not because I read it somewhere, but because I hear it all the time from those who attend my classes and seminars and those I coach, from my corporate clients, and from the countless letters and emails I receive from those who've read my books and articles in newspapers and magazines as well as those who've heard me speak.

I'm a business communications trainer and coach. I have been teaching business etiquette for more than fifteen years. I give approximately one hundred seminars and coaching sessions a year to a wide range of business professionals at all rungs on the corporate ladder. They come from a wide variety of companies—large and small—and from all across the country as well as from overseas. I've also taught in numerous countries including Kuwait, France, and Mexico, which has given me insight into our increasingly global business environment.

My clients include some of the world's leading business and financial players, like NASA, Pfizer Inc., and DaimlerChrysler. They hire the best and the brightest. Yet I have seen promising, even brilliant, careers derailed, sidetracked, or blown sky-high, simply because people made mistakes—in meetings, at business meals, on the telephone, at the office holiday party, when they got dressed in the morning, in the emails they sent, while giving a presentation . . . the list goes on and on.

Take the woman who answered her cell phone during a job interview and proceeded to conduct a conversation with her kids. Until that moment, the job was hers; after the phone call, the offer disappeared. And what about the salesperson who feigned a heart attack to get his customer's attention? He lost the customer as a result. Or the programmer who was trimming his fingernails during a meeting—one of his clippings went flying into the air. He leaned over and asked the woman next to him, "That didn't go into your coffee, did it?" He was no longer asked to meetings.

If you think I've made these stories up or that I am exaggerating them, I can guarantee that I am not. I am an irresistible force when it comes to attracting bad behavior stories. People love sharing their horror stories with me. Bosses tell me what their employees do and employees share with me what their bosses do.

What You Don't Know Really Can Hurt You

Before you think I am being harsh, let me set the record straight: I know most people don't set out to be jerks, and I am willing to extend the benefit of the doubt to all of those blunderers barging through life with bewilderingly bad behavior. I know that, in most cases, they are simply oblivious to the way others view their behavior. I know that they don't even think about establishing rapport with the person across the table at the conference or on the other end of the phone as they are multitasking. It's true and unfortunate for them that they're not thinking—at least, not thinking about the consequences of their actions—because, in most cases, they are the ones whose careers will be put on hold by their behavior.

I've witnessed and heard it too many times from professionals whose careers have been stalled or derailed completely not to believe it—all of your actions have consequences, especially those that make others stop and say, "What the heck was she thinking?" or, "Do I really want to work or do business with him?!"

Business professionals often limit their success because of the way they behave, how they present themselves, or what they do—or don't—say. More often than not, as the following examples demonstrate, they don't even know that they are doing so.

- *A strategic planner wheeled around after a colleague held the door for her and read him the riot act.*

- *After spending the afternoon in a meeting with a female colleague, the marketing manager called her at home that night. He was furious that she hadn't told him his fly was open.*

- *An automotive parts buyer couldn't understand why her local Japanese supplier wouldn't accept her business proposal. She had put off visiting him and he didn't want to work with her until he had met her.*

These real-life examples are telling illustrations of what can happen to any of us as we go about the business of doing business. They also illustrate the variety of issues that fall under the broad banner of "business etiquette." Just knowing which fork to use won't cut the mustard (so to speak) in today's business environment. Even things men and women would have taken for granted, say, twenty years ago, can't be taken for granted today. Who back then would have thought for example that a man would get chewed out by a woman simply for holding a door open? Sounds a bit extreme, but don't laugh, it happens! What should a man—or a woman, for that matter—do in such a situation? *NewRules@Work* clues you in on that and a great deal more of the dos and don'ts of business etiquette.

In today's business environment, etiquette is not just a matter of being polite. More than ever, each of us must know how to maximize those social skills that give us the confidence to handle people and situations with tact, diplomacy, and respect; essential skills that help us avoid business blunders that can cause embarrassment, discomfort, or worse—as our poor consultant learned—cost us the relationship, business opportunity, account, client, promotion, or our job.

Knowing a lot about your area of expertise isn't always enough to move you up the organizational chart. Of course, you have to know your field and do your job well. However, it takes more than that in today's highly competitive workplace. And that's where etiquette comes in. The ability to get along with others, demonstrate good manners, and make others feel comfortable is increasingly important. Without these skills, business can be lost, your voice won't be heard at meetings, your staff can lose respect for you, and your managers won't promote you. A polite, professional manner is a key component of how successful you will be.

To those just entering the workplace, the idea of "business etiquette" may seem quaint. It's not a subject taught much in school these days. Few high schools, colleges, or universities offer courses in business etiquette. Yet good manners are vital not only to the smooth functioning of today's fast-paced workplace, they help prevent misunderstandings and wounded feelings; they alleviate tension and reduce stress. Good manners can soften the high-pressure demands we place on our coworkers and forestall explosive outbursts. It seems so obvious; yet, in today's hectic, bottom line–oriented business environment, many of us become so absorbed in getting the job done that we sometimes forget the lessons we learned as youngsters.

At the same time, etiquette does not stand still. Good business etiquette must change with the times. Fifty years ago, most women would have *expected* men to hold doors open for them, and most etiquette books would have advised men to do so. Manners need updating not only to keep place with changes in the workforce, as well as with changes in society, but also to keep pace with changes in technology. More and more, we communicate by email or voicemail—useful but often impersonal tools that actually *increase* the need for politeness. Yet, all too often in the real world manners are totally forgotten. Greetings may go by the board; pleases and thank-yous are eliminated in favor of brevity; silence replaces kind words.

For those who do business internationally, or hope to, knowledge of other cultures can help you distinguish between behavior that is proper in one culture and offensive in another. Even in the most casual and laid-back office environment, etiquette is essential to a smooth-running operation. It need not be formal, but it needs to be there.

What This Book Will Do for You

NewRules@Work takes a totally new, fun, and fast approach to helping you get and stay ahead career-wise. By emphasizing only the essentials of business etiquette and communications, you can turn to the specific information you need and put it to work immediately.

I know from experience that real-life blunders make the point much better than I can ever hope to. I've seen it time and again as I work with professionals at all levels and in all fields. They remember the mistakes of others because they're often outrageous, funny, or just plain hard to forget. I know that's true and I've seen firsthand the impact they have on others.

I can tell someone, for example, not to get drunk at a business lunch. This is sound advice. I know it, you know it, and I'm certain those attending my seminars understand how important this simple rule is; yet I can practically guarantee that they'll all remember the point more vividly when they hear about the account representative who threw up on his client after taking him to a ballgame.

That's why this book is filled with true stories ripped from my files.

You'll also find Pachter's Pointers, techniques I've learned over the years, which will help steer you through some of the finer points of business etiquette; and Quick Tips offer handy ideas on related topics. The Blunder Busters sprinkled throughout offer readers additional information, guidance, and advice about such things as how to recover from an "innocent" mistake, rebuild your professional image, and recover from an embarrassing gaffe.

In *NewRules@Work* we'll explore everything from business dining, to dressing for a presentation, to writing an effective email. If you read the book from cover to cover, you'll find all the essentials you'll ever need to know about business etiquette. But, if you just want a quick tip on:

- What to do in an all-important business meeting with a new boss, dive into "Making the Most of Meetings" in Part Five.

- Job interview problems? Go to tip #70: Be prepared for the interview to find out how to polish up your skills.

- How to handle a sticky email? Take a peek at the section in Part Four called "Before You Press 'Send': Email Embarrassments and Other Faux Pas."

- How about speaking well of yourself? Pick up tips in #56, which will show you how to master the fine art of self-promotion.

- Unsure about how to shake hands? Go to tips #7 and #8.

- Need to learn how to mingle? Take a look at tip #28 and find eight ways to become a mingling maven.

- Uncertain whether your clothing is appropriate for work? Dive into tips #32 to #35, where you'll get up-to-the-minute guidelines on professional and casual dress.

Whatever the situation, you'll find the solution—*before* you make that big blunder.

PART ONE

The Inside Scoop: Making Connections and Establishing Rapport

First impressions really do count. Most people want to do business with people they know, like, and trust. Your ability to interact graciously and politely from the moment you meet someone sets the stage for everything that follows.

Little things say a lot, and it is often the small courtesies that are *so* easy to do, but *so* easy to overlook, that make the biggest difference. A small gesture often tells a person—whether it's a colleague, a boss, a client, or a customer—more about you, more quickly, than your entire résumé. It shows that you are thoughtful and concerned; it expresses competence as well as warmth; and it may even signal that you are a person of character.

It stands to reason then, that forgetting these little things does the opposite. It can make you appear inconsiderate, rude, and, worse, offensive. Omit the little things at your peril: You can destroy relationships. You can alienate customers. You can decimate your reputation. You can lose business. And, beyond all of this, it's just not very nice to treat others poorly!

Establishing an initial connection with others is one of the most important "little" things that a person can do—in life as well as in business. It may seem strange, but *how* you say hello, whether or not you say hello or introduce someone, tells a person a great deal about you. And, although we think we do all these things correctly, many of us have trouble doing them.

Nowhere is connecting with others more important than in a work situation. Since a smooth beginning can pave the way to strong, lasting relationships with everyone you encounter in business—in and outside your company—we'll start there. But before we dive in, take a few minutes and give yourself this short quiz.

Test Yourself:
Where Are You on the Relationship Track?

	TRUE	FALSE
1. It's important to say "hello" or "good morning" to people you know as well as to those you don't know when walking around at work.	☐	☐
2. In the United States, a man no longer needs to wait for a woman to extend her hand before extending his.	☐	☐
3. I always respond when someone greets me at work.	☐	☐

	TRUE	FALSE
4. I stand up before shaking someone's hand.	☐	☐
5. The following is a proper introduction: "Ms. Smith (the customer), I'd like you to meet my manager, Mr. Jones."	☐	☐
6. I carry business cards with me at all times.	☐	☐
7. I don't avoid someone if I forget his or her name.	☐	☐
8. Before I enter a room, I move anything I am carrying into my left hand.	☐	☐
9. I pin my name tag on my right side.	☐	☐

Your answers to all the questions should be true! If they were, that's great, but wait; don't skip to the next part. Read on to find out *why* they are true. Understanding the reasons behind your actions will make it much easier to remember to put them into practice, even when you find yourself in the midst of a difficult situation.

"Hello, Hello, Hello . . .": The First Step

Debbie joined the accounting department of a big wholesaler. She reported to Tom, the accounts receivable manager. About a week into the job, Tom asked Debbie to prepare a report on the aging of the receivables. Tom was so impressed with her work that he said, "This is a great time for you to get to know my boss, John, the head of the whole department." She was pleased and excited that Tom trusted her with this important task and that she had done so well that he was letting her "take credit for it." She set up an appointment and arrived promptly. On entering John's office she said, "Hi, John. We only met briefly before, I'm—" Before she had a chance to finish, he snapped, *"I don't need to greet you, just give me the damn report."* She did, and quickly retreated.

What Went Wrong?

John missed a great opportunity to get to know a promising staff member and to set a tone for his department. Debbie's not going to forget that moment easily. It may color her view of the department and company. No matter how high your position in a company is, greetings are crucial first steps in establishing rapport. Whether you are the boss greeting a staff member and making her feel welcome, a sales clerk greeting a customer warmly, or an account executive confidently meeting a new client, you immediately establish a connection. It's as if you were saying, "I see you. I connect with you. You are part of my day, if only for a brief moment."

BLUNDER BUSTER

Practice W-A-T (Walk Around Time) for ten minutes in the morning and five minutes in the afternoon. Greet those you meet along the way. If you're the boss, you'll have no problem; you may even want to poke your head into someone's office occasionally to commend them or just to have a quick catch-up conversation. If you're lower down the corporate ladder, you may have to do it en route to the copier or the coffee room. Don't overdo it, but do do it.

People in my seminars often tell me that one of the things they most dislike is when others fail to greet or acknowledge them. Yet it happens all the time. Debbie was new to the company and wanted to make a good impression. John's response said, "I don't care about you or what you've done." Debbie was not an aggressive salesperson pressuring John to purchase the latest computer system; she was simply offering a greeting—a friendly "hello." John may have been harried, he may have been rushed, but in the same time it took him to be rude and throw a wet blanket on Debbie, he could have said, "Welcome aboard. I was in a hurry for this report; thanks so much for delivering it personally."

If that's not enough to convince you, then think about the consequences. One of my clients surveyed their company's employees and discovered that the employees judged a manager's effectiveness by whether or not the manager greeted and acknowledged them.

I coached a woman who had been demoted from director to senior manager. Many things led to this, but one of them was that she couldn't motivate her staff or gain the cooperation of the people she worked with. Her boss told me that she never said anything to anyone unless it was "strictly business." I can't describe how astonished (and delighted) she was to discover how much more helpful her colleagues became after she began greeting them.

1. Which greeting should you use?

"Hey" is not a corporate greeting. Neither is "Yo!" That may be pretty obvious, but did you know that not only are there greetings that shouldn't be used in a professional setting, there is a hierarchy of greetings, ranging from very informal to formal, that are appropriate in different situations. Some of these—in order of formality—are:

Hi
Hello
Good morning
Good afternoon
Good evening

I once taught etiquette to the staff of a private club. The manager wanted to raise the club's image to attract more members to use the facilities for business as well as personal entertaining. We decided to begin by training all the club's employees to greet club members with the formal, "Good morning, Mr. Jones." It was subtle, but it worked. Membership increased.

▶ **QUICK TIP:** There are nonverbal greetings: the smile, the nod, and the wave. Use them if, for some reason, it's awkward to speak or you are in a hurry (or you notice the other person is) or you keep passing the same person in a short amount of time.

Pachter's Pointer: "Hi, how are you?" is not a question . . .

It's a greeting, and in the United States the only response to this statement is "Fine, thank you," or, "I'm well. How are you?" This is not the time to go into all the details of your health.

This is not unusual: The French use *"Comment ça va?"* ("How's it going?") in much the same way we do; the British greeting "How do you do?" is rhetorical; and a typical Chinese greeting dating back hundreds, perhaps thousands, of years translates roughly to "Have you eaten?" dating from the times when food was scarce. They don't, of course, expect a literal answer.

2. Observe yourself. Do you do say hello when . . .

1. *You run into people you know.* This sounds so obvious yet people don't do it. In one of my classes, I tell students to tune in and really watch their greeting habits. Many are surprised to discover that although they thought they had said hello to everyone (in fact, they thought they had made it a point to say hello to everyone), they really hadn't. A woman in one recent seminar returned from lunch break shocked to discover she hadn't greeted two people on the way back to the seminar. She was certain she'd always greeted everyone. Just reminding yourself to greet people will help you remember to do it automatically.

Pachter's Pointer: When You See Someone, SES them.

S = Smile.
E = Eye contact. Look at the person.
S = Say something. "Hello," "Good morning," or "How are

you?" You can also add a comment; for example, "Nice day, isn't it?"

You will be amazed at how people respond to you when you make SESing them a habit.

Forgetting a name is no excuse . . .

If you say hello with a smile on your face, more often than not people never even realize that you didn't greet them by name.

2. *You encounter people you* don't *know.* The advice "don't talk to strangers" may be true if you happen to be in a dark alley, but it won't get you ahead in corporate America. A greeting doesn't have to be a big deal; as we said, just a nod, a smile, or a "good morning," is usually sufficient.

One executive VP I know never said hello to anyone until an administrative assistant was assigned to him. After their first meeting, she said, "You know, I was afraid to talk to you, but now that I am working for you, I am no longer afraid." Surprised, he asked why. The AA replied, "Before I worked for you, you never said hello." From that moment on, the VP made it a point to greet everyone he encountered.

Pachter's Pointer: Friendly rewards.

A friend of mine, a consultant, often worked for a large corporation. She made it a habit always to smile and say hello to anyone she encountered. She frequently ran into a man she did not know. One day he stopped her in the hallway and asked for her résumé. It turned out he was the head of the HR department. Sure enough, a few days later he called and offered her a job she couldn't refuse. As she put it, she was "hired because she said hello." It never hurts to be friendly, and, who knows, you might even be offered a great job!

3. *Someone greets you.* You *must* respond. It is not optional!

You would not believe how many people tell me that they are frequently ignored when they say hello to colleagues they encounter in hallways, elevators, cafeterias, and elsewhere in the office.

Not too long ago, a woman attending a seminar said she was so tired of saying hello only to find most people unresponsive that she was going to stop doing it. I couldn't have planned it better: Another attendee immediately turned to her and said, "No, please keep on saying hello. I'm a new employee, and it really makes a big difference to me when folks say hello."

Pachter's Pointer: Observe the 10 to 5 rule.

People ask, at what point do I say hello? What if the person is down the hall, across the way? I learned the following guideline from a resort in Phoenix that I think will help answer the question: If you make eye contact with someone who is within ten feet of you, you *must* acknowledge the person with a nod or a smile. At five feet you *must* say something: "Hello," or "Good morning." A women in my seminar said that her company uses the 10 to 4 rule.

This is a really good suggestion because it drives people crazy when someone pretends they don't see them!

"You Can Call Me Sam, You Can Call Me Joe . . .": Introducing Yourself in a Crowd

Colin, the VP of marketing, joined a group of employees at the company's holiday reception. He simply entered the group, said hi to the group, and started talking as if he knew everyone. Jerry, who had recently joined the company as a member of the research team, had never met Colin. Jerry felt awkward interrupting, and didn't introduce himself. Throughout the conversation, he felt invisible and, although he had some good ideas, didn't contribute them. This was unfortunate because he lost an opportunity to make a good impression.

What Went Wrong?

It would have been nice if Colin realized that Jerry was part of the group and recognized that he didn't know him and introduced himself. But in the real world, that often doesn't happen. There are situations where you *must* introduce yourself. And for Jerry, this was one of them. In fact, introducing oneself is so common that this type of introduction even has a name; it is called the *self-introduction* and you should use it if you are:

- *Initiating a connection with someone you don't know.* If you don't do it, it may not happen.

- *In a group of strangers* or mostly strangers where each person is introducing him- or herself.

BLUNDER BUSTER

Try again.

Jerry can't retrieve this moment, but there are ways to recover momentum. At some convenient point in the evening, he can introduce himself to Colin. If Colin is alone, he might even add:

"I heard you talking earlier. I'm Jerry Jones, and I've been thinking about it; what if . . ."

- *In a group where the participants know one another* and did not think to introduce you—the situation Jerry found himself in. Instead of saying nothing, Jerry could have said:

    Hi, I'm Jerry Jones. I just joined the company as an analyst in the research department. It's a pleasure to meet you.

3. Five steps to a successful self-introduction.

1. *Keep it short.* Say your name and, in a sentence or two, what type of work you do.

2. *Tailor it to the event.*

    "I'm Barbara Pachter, the speaker for tonight's program."

    "I'm Barbara Pachter, the author of NewRules@Work."

3. *Speak clearly and slowly.* Remember, you want the other person to remember your name, so don't talk so quickly that people do not understand you.

4. *Prepare your introduction.* I know that may sound silly; after all you know your name, right? Yes, but you may get flustered

or feel awkward, just as Jerry did. If you prepare, you won't get caught off guard. Before you walk into an event, whether it's a meeting with clients, your new boss, a conference, or a gala, decide how you will introduce yourself.

5. *Shake hands after introducing yourself.* Later in this chapter, we'll talk about how to shake hands.

 Pachter's Pointer: Don't sit at a table without introducing yourself.

When you're seated at a table, introduce yourself to everyone at the table. If that's not possible, introduce yourself to those on either side of you. Don't wait for the other person to do it. Just say hi or hello and state your name.

"Have You Met What's-Her-Name?": Effortless Introductions

Michael, an accountant at a prestigious firm, took a client, George, out to dinner. Sarah, also a client of Michael's, happened to be in the same restaurant, and came over to the table to talk to him. The conversation lasted several minutes, but Michael never introduced Sarah. George sat there, without saying a word, but became increasingly upset as the conversation went on. When Sarah left, Michael noticed a chill in the air. When he asked George if something was the matter, George blurted out, "How come you didn't introduce me to that woman?" Michael confessed that he had forgotten her name.

What Went Wrong?

Introducing people to one another sounds so simple, doesn't it? "Ms. Smith, this is Mr. Jones." Easy as pie, you would think, but things can go wrong, and when they do they can ruin what might otherwise have been a perfect business relationship. As Michael learned the hard way, even in an established relationship, not introducing a third person can create bad feelings.

It is your responsibility to make the introduction if you are the:

- host

- person in charge

- person who knows both people

BLUNDER BUSTER

When you forget someone's name:

1. *Admit it.* It happens to us all. Use a simple, polite line, but don't overdo it. No need to keep saying, "I'm sorry, I'm so sorry. I can't believe this. You must be so upset with me. I am really sorry." Just say something simple:

    "I'm sorry; I've forgotten your name."

    "We've met before, but I'm afraid I've forgotten your name."

    "Please forgive me. I've never been good with names."

2. *Bluff:* You can try this, and hope that one or both jump in.

    "Have you met my boss, Mindy Cola?"

    "Have you two met?"

    But, beware if they don't, it can be awkward.

3. *Dramatize it:* You can, if you're the type to carry it off, create a distraction so you don't have to make the introduction. Doug, on the TV show *King of Queens*, feigned a heart attack during his wife's office party rather than admit he'd forgotten someone's name. I don't recommend this.

Michael was clearly the host—and, at least in theory, knew both people's names. It was his responsibility to make an introduction or to say something.

As a rule, if you are not introduced, don't stand on ceremony; introduce yourself. Once you have made eye contact, say something like,

"I'm Julie Suarez. I don't believe we have met."

"I'm Richard Harrison, and you are . . . ?"

If you think the person who neglected to introduce you will be embarrassed by this, you may not want to do it, but more often than not, he might be relieved that you've realized his dilemma and that you've taken him off the hook!

4. Introductions made simple.

Introductions can seem complicated, but following these guidelines will make them very easy.

1. *Say the name of the most important person first.* Yes, regardless of gender. It used to be that women's names were said first; that is no longer the case.

   "Ms. Greater Importance, I would like you to meet Mr. Lesser Importance."

   "Tom Camper (the client), I would like you to meet our purchasing agent, Mary Smith."

   For obvious reasons, the client is considered the more important person!

   And don't seesaw back and forth:

   "Tom Jones, this is Mary Smith. Mary Smith, this is Tom Jones."

   Once is enough! And remember, first names alone won't do it. They don't provide enough information.

▶ **QUICK TIP:** If you don't know who is most important, name the person you want to flatter first.

 Pachter's Pointer: A bad introduction is usually better than no introduction.

Make introductions. Most people won't remember whether their name was said first or second, but they *will* remember whether or not they were introduced.

2. *Say something about the person.* Not a lot, just enough to provide a springboard for conversation.

> *"Bill Smith, this is Tom Jones. He just joined our company from ABC organization. Bill is the head of the new marketing program."*

5. What to say after you are introduced.

A simple response and usually a handshake (see pages 20–22) are all that is required. Possible responses include:

> *"How do you do?"*
> *"Pleased to meet you."*
> *"Nice meeting you."*

Name-Calling Calamities and How to Avoid Them

John was leaving the department and, as a joke, Suzanne signed the farewell card, "Your Cupcake, Suzanne." Her colleagues saw it and could not resist. From then on, she was "Cupcake." She hated it.

What Went Wrong?

What was Suzanne thinking? Yes, of course, there's no doubt that she brought all the teasing on herself. Still, sexist nicknames are not okay at work—under any circumstances. In fact, using any nickname—even one that isn't sexist—is a no-no if the person doesn't use it.

6. What's in a name? A lot!

People are very fussy about what you do to their names. This is true whether you are addressing the person face-to-face or in writing.

1. *Never use sexist nicknames.* It is amazing what people have been called. "Hon," "doll," "cupcake," "sweetie," "babycakes," "toots," "sunshine," "darlin'," and "sexy lady" have all been used at work! One supervisor thanked the women on his staff for their help on a rush project with, "Thanks, Chicklets." You can imagine how well that went over.

2. *Do not shorten a person's name,* unless you know it's okay to do so. My friend Robert doesn't like being called Rob and

never uses it; still, some people persist in calling him Rob. He mostly ignores it, but he doesn't like it.

Some Barbaras (I'm one) may not want to be called Barb, and Richard may not want to be Dick or Rick or Rich. Think twice before you give someone a moniker they don't want or like.

Using your full name suggests a more professional image. Nicknames like Ritchie, Suzie, or Willie connote a young person. A professor in a prominent MBA program told her students to call her Margie. One day, she overheard a student say, "Oh, like 'My Little Margie' is going to care if I hand this in late."

3. *When in doubt, ask.* If you don't know what to call someone, ask him, "Is it all right if I call you Joe?"

One CEO came up with creative way to let people know what to call him. When he joined the company, he sent this email to the entire staff:

> *What should you say when we meet in the elevator? Good*
> *morning (check one):*
> ☐ *Dr. Jones*
> ☐ *Mr. Jones*
> ☐ *John*

The correct answer: Good morning, John.

Pachter's Pointer: First names, last names . . .

In many companies, particularly in the United States, people are on a first-name basis. This can cause confusion, sometimes with humorous results. In one instance, a German company merged with an American company and was holding its first joint training session. Before the session, the German participants were told to address their counterparts using their first names, in deference to American informality. You can probably guess the punch line: Of course, the Americans were advised to use surnames when dealing with their new counterparts to accommodate German custom. They all laughed a lot when they discovered what happened.

Learn your company's protocols, and, when in doubt or when you meet people from other countries for the first time, use last names.

And on a related subject: Most people now know that Ms. is the preferred term in business and understand that it does not designate marital status. If you are asked to use Mrs. or Miss, by all means do; at other times choose Ms.

"Not Too Hard, Not Too Soft—Just Right": Shaking Hands Correctly

Joanne was interviewing for a job. She and the interviewer shook hands. The interviewer squeezed. She squeezed back a little harder, he then squeezed harder; she squeezed harder still. That's when she realized she had lost the job!

What Went Wrong?

Shaking hands is not a competitive sport! In the United States, a handshake is proper business protocol, and if you want to be taken seriously, you must shake hands.

We make judgments about people based on the quality of their handshake. Numerous people have told me that they decided not to do business with someone based solely on that person's limp handshake. An executive I coached who'd come through every stage of the interview process with flying colors almost didn't get the job because, the recruiter later told him, his handshake was "like mush."

7. Shaking hands is more than two hands touching.

An impressive handshake takes:

1. *Two feet.* Stand up when you shake someone's hand. Yes, there are times when you can't get up, but you can demonstrate that you would, if you could, and you know you should!

2. *Eye contact.* Look at the person and give him or her your full attention. Don't look around; don't look over or past the person; it gives the impression that you don't really care.

3. *Speech.* Say your name as you extend your hand.

4. *Your hand.* Go in with the thumb up and have thumb joints meet.

▶ **QUICK TIP:** A handshake should be firm, but not bone-breaking. Two to three pumps does it.

8. When to shake hands.

The president of a large company makes it a point to greet each participant and shake his or her hand before every meeting. They love him!

You should be certain to shake hands when you:

- Greet someone with more than just a hello *and* when you say goodbye.

- Are introduced to someone.

- Are visited in your office by someone from outside the company; for example, a customer, client, or vendor.

- Encounter a business colleague outside the office.

- Feel it is appropriate. Trust me; you'll develop a sixth sense for when it is.

Greetings and Gender:
Handshakes Are for Women, Too

A woman attending one of my seminars told me about a time she was the only woman participating in a meeting. When the attendees were introduced to the chairman, he shook hands with all the men, but did not extend his hand to her. At the time, she was young and a bit intimidated and did nothing about it, but it made her feel invisible for the rest of the day. Looking back on it, she realized that she, too, hadn't extended her hand.

What Went Wrong?

The handshake is not a gender greeting. Both men and women should shake hands—men with men and women, women with women and men.

Many women have never been taught to shake hands. As a result, some women feel uncomfortable shaking hands, especially with other women. When we discussed this phenomenon at another seminar, a high-powered corporate lawyer confessed, "You're right. I never thought about it, but I am not teaching my four-year-old daughter to shake hands, although I've started teaching my son, and he's only two!"

Both men and women also should stand when introduced. In my seminars, when I introduce myself to each of the participants, I've noticed that approximately 75 percent of the men stand; only 35 percent of the women do. This not only violates the rules of shaking hands, but not standing can make you seem invisible or, at minimum, less important. A CEO of a Fortune 100 company went around the room introducing himself to the three women and one man attending a meeting. He had a conversation with just one person—the only person who stood (who just happened to be a man)! We are sometimes too quick to think that men just opt to talk to men, and that may at times be true, but in this case I am more inclined to believe that it was because the man stood.

 Pachter's Pointer: Keep your right hand free.

Before you enter a room, move anything you may be holding from your right hand to your left. That way, you won't fumble around when someone wants to shake your hand.

A word to the wise: Wear your name tag on your right shoulder. It makes it easier for people to see your name when you shake hands.

9. Gender myths.

1. *A man should wait for a woman to extend her hand.* There was a time when this was true, but not any more in the United States. The higher-ranking person should extend his or her hand first, but since there is still a lot of confusion in the workplace about shaking hands, it's a good idea to give the higher-ranking person a split-second before you extend your hand. If he or she still has not extended a hand, extend yours. The important thing is that you shake hands. Outside the United States, men may still need to wait for the woman to extend her hand. Before you go, check the Internet or books on international business etiquette to learn the customs of the country you will be visiting.

2. *A kiss is rarely appropriate.* A handshake is the proper business greeting for business *and* business social situations. As a rule, kissing is off-limits, but there are some occasions where a kiss may be appropriate. Here are a few guidelines, but the best advice is: When in doubt, don't.

- *The type of company you work for.* Large, formal, or conservative companies usually have less kissing than smaller, creative, or informal types of companies.

- *Your relationship with the person.* If people know each other well, they may kiss at business social events.

- *The type of business functions you attend.* Company picnics are more relaxed and informal than business meetings or dinners at a fancy restaurant.

▶ **QUICK TIP:** Be prepared. In many countries—particularly in Europe—you may encounter a great deal of kissing; actually touching cheeks and kissing the air. Arab men may also exchange kisses on each cheek.

Pachter's Pointer: A kiss is not always *just* a kiss.

> A young, attractive, pharmaceutical sales representative would kiss her physician-customers when she saw them in their offices. One day, at a dinner meeting, she greeted a doctor with a big kiss in front of his wife. Neither was pleased.

10. What to do if you don't shake hands.

Among certain followers of Islam and Orthodox Judaism, men are not allowed to touch adult women who are not their wives. Some people with disabilities have difficulty shaking hands or rising when they are introduced.

If for these or any other reason you are unable to shake a person's hand:

1. *Explain.* If you are unable to shake hands, say something polite, such as, "I am so sorry. My religion does not permit it."

2. *Make an exception for work situations, if you can.* One Muslim woman I know said that she did shake hands with men at work. It was too awkward not to, she explained, but in her social life, she did not do it.

   When I was teaching in the Middle East, a couple of my students covered their hand with their sleeve when we shook hands, so we were not touching flesh to flesh.

The Business of Business Cards

At a networking event, Sam, a salesman, gave a potential client his business card, or so he thought. A few moments later, the client returned the card, with the icy comment, "You probably want to keep this one," and walked away. Sam had given her a card he received earlier at a lunch meeting. On the back of it he had written some notes—fat, bald, small eyes, double chin—to remind him of the person.

What Went Wrong?

Good idea, bad execution! It is often helpful to write notes on the back of a person's card, but make sure no one sees them!

11. Your card talks . . .

Your business card says a lot about you. Business cards are an easy way to provide your "vital statistics" quickly and compactly. How they look and feel—especially if you are self-employed—is often as important as the information they provide. Big corporations have their own style, but regardless of the style, how you treat them is important.

1. *The case counts.* Make sure your card case is in good shape and in an easy-to-reach place.

2. *Update your card regularly.* Don't cross anything out or hand-write new information. Be cautious with computer-generated cards. Make sure they have a professional look and feel.

BLUNDER BUSTER

While this won't save Sam, it's always a good idea to separate your own cards from those you receive. Some people put cards they receive in one part of their card case and those they give out in the other. Some use separate, different-looking card cases. Still others use different jacket pockets.

3. *Keep them handy.* Wherever you go, your card case should go with you. You don't have to give them out, nor should you plan on emptying half a box per event, but you never know when someone might ask for one (even at a social event).

4. *Exchange cards at the end of the meeting.* In the United States, if you are meeting with just one person, this is usually done at the end of a meeting. However, you can exchange cards at the beginning if you are meeting with more than one person.

▶ **QUICK TIP:** The Japanese custom of placing each person's card on the table opposite the person can help you remember that person's name.

5. *Internationally, the exchange of cards can be an important ritual.* In Japan, exchanging cards is part of the initial greeting. People bow, say, "Good morning," and exchange cards with two hands. That means you are giving it with full measure. The card tells a lot about the person. Look at the card when you receive it, acknowledge it. Don't be casual with it. It represents the person.

In the Middle East (Arab world), cards are exchanged with the right hand only. The left hand is considered unclean.

What to Say, When: Selecting Topics for Conversation

Steve, a lawyer from Chicago was coming to Philadelphia to handle a court case. He flew first-class and during the flight chatted with the man next to him, who asked Steve why he was coming to town. Steve replied that he was working on a case, and that his opponent was some "bozo from Philadelphia." The man asked questions; they continued to talk and Steve proceeded to lay out his whole strategy for the case. The next morning in the courtroom, Steve was tapped on the shoulder. He turned around to hear, "Hi. I'm the bozo from Philadelphia."

What Went Wrong?

It was foolish of Steve to have discussed the case, and, as it turned out, the mistake was costly to him (and to his client). It's not a good idea to discuss business strategy in public places and it's *never* a good idea to discuss it with strangers! In this case, Steve unknowingly gave vital information to the man next to him, but even if that wasn't the case, those around them may also have overheard the conversation and benefitted from it.

12. Topics to avoid.

1. *Personal subjects.* As you get to know a business acquaintance better, you may want to share some information about yourself—you're married, you have children, your hobbies, your

husband's a chiropractor. But some subjects should remain out of bounds. For example, I know of a young woman who told her customer that someone else would be handling her account. That should have been enough, but she went on to say that she was getting married in six days because her birth control hadn't worked and now she was pregnant. That stopped the conversation cold. Her customer was uncomfortable and did not know how to respond. If something is very intimate, in business, remember the old adage, "Better safe than sorry," and keep it to yourself. This actually works both ways; don't solicit very personal information about colleagues, clients, customers, etc.

2. *Sex, politics, or religion.* As a rule, whether it's business or personal, you don't want to offend anyone, and these are the "Big Three" of topics you should steer clear of; people often have strong feelings about each of them. Rather than put your foot in your mouth, it's best not to venture into any of these areas.

3. *Strategy and tactics.* At least, not with strangers, and not in places where you can be overheard. I know I'm repeating myself, but I can't say it too often. By the way, this is especially true when you are talking on a cell phone. People tend to believe they are having a private conversation (at the same time, they tend to talk louder than usual), but you never know who may overhear you and what use they could make of the information.

13. What's left to talk about?

Appropriate topics include movies, sports (if everyone involved in the conversation is interested), family (if everyone is interested), food, current events (cautiously), vacations, holiday plans, the environment you are in, and the weather—especially front-page weather.

Pictures or certificates on display in someone's office can open broad areas of conversation. If you see a picture of a girl in a soccer uniform on someone's desk, for example, saying something like, "My son also plays soccer" or "Soccer's a really good sport for kids" can pave the way for further discussion.

Little Things Mean a Lot: Making Small Talk

At a get-to-know-you offsite meeting, there was a lot of conversation about the recent devastating tsunami. Karen, who was new to the company, was eager to make a good impression and perhaps even get to chair one of the committees the group would be setting up. She had immersed herself in preparation for the meeting, and hadn't looked at the paper or watched TV news for a week. Rather than admit ignorance, she just sat there and didn't say a word, thereby missing a glorious opportunity for the team to get to know her and for her to get to know them. Although she participated in the sessions and said some smart things, her hopes for chairing vanished.

What Went Wrong?

If you don't have anything to say, it's difficult to connect with others. When you meet new people, small talk helps them to get to know you and you to know them. It allows them to see how you interact with other people. By not participating, Karen's new colleagues may have thought she was a snob, or timid, or hiding something. They may even have thought that she'd be hard to work with, and, therefore, not the right person to chair a committee.

14. Tips for making small talk.

1. *Demonstrate interest.* A good way to do this is to listen to what the person has to say.

2. *Prepare.* You will feel much more comfortable when you have something to say. Read newspapers or news magazines or watch the TV news and talk shows so you'll know what's going on in the world. Read professional journals and newsletters so you'll know what's going on in your field. Keep abreast of any special events that might be happening in your city or the city you're visiting.

3. *Pay attention.* When talking with someone, give that person your undivided attention. Don't interrupt. Maintain eye contact. Most people hate talking with someone who is looking everywhere except at them.

4. *Ask questions.* To encourage the conversation, ask open-ended questions that require more than a yes or no or other simple answer. Instead of asking, "How long have you been with your company?" or "Are you a member of this organization?" you might say, "You seem so knowledgeable; what's your background?" or "How did you get involved with this group?"

5. *Be open.* Let people get to know you better. You need to reveal a little about yourself in order to have things to talk about. Again, what you reveal doesn't have to be very personal, but sharing your interests allows you to establish some common ground, which, in turn, can lead to conversation.

The New Rules of "Helping Etiquette"

Marta, a strategic planner, was heading off to a meeting with the COO. Thomas, who was going in the opposite direction, stopped and waited and held the door for her. Instead of the "thank you" he anticipated, Marta wheeled around and read him the riot act!

What Went Wrong?

Marta was just plain rude. Yes, men are no longer required to open the door for women, but she was just rude. And I am not talking solely about the fact that she exploded, which is never appropriate, I'm talking about her overreaction. Marta didn't want help with the door, but the level of her reaction does not fit the crime of a door held open.

One of the changes in the workplace over the last thirty years has been ever increasing number of women in the workplace and their increased level of responsibility. Women fought hard for this, and can feel slighted when they are treated differently than a man would be in the same situation.

In our social lives, it's still not uncommon for men to help women and pay deference to them simply because they are women (although even this has changed and is changing). In the workplace, helping a woman in a circumstance in which you wouldn't help a man may undermine—even inadvertently—her credibility. The new gender-free "manners" guideline is, whenever possible, not to base decisions about how men and women interact on gender but on host/visitor status, rank, or reciprocal kindness.

BLUNDER BUSTER

And speaking of doors . . .

I have taught etiquette for a number of years to tens of thousands of people. In my experience—with no disrespect to men—men have no difficulty giving up paying the bills, or carrying the packages, or helping a woman with her coat, but for some reason that no man has ever been able to fully explain, men want to open doors for women. They just do.

My advice: Let them! If a man opens a door for you, simply turn around and say, "Thank you."

---

15. How may I help?

The rules for:

1. *Paying the bill:* The host does the inviting and the host pays the bill, regardless of gender.

2. *Carrying the packages:* Help anyone who needs help, regardless of gender.

3. *Helping with a coat:* Ditto.

4. *Pulling out chairs:* Yes, men and women can pull out their own chairs, but of course help anyone who needs help.

5. *Opening a door:* Whoever reaches the door first opens it and holds it for the next person. It is rude to let a door close in someone's face. It is also a very smart junior staffer or gracious host who *subtly* maneuvers to get to the door first and opens it

for the senior person or guest—but make sure you don't trip
anyone in your rush to the exit!

 Pachter's Pointer: You can't have it both ways.

> In a recent seminar with employees at a major organization
> we quickly reviewed these gender guidelines. When we got
> to the one about picking up a check, a woman said she
> agreed with everything, *except* that. She wanted men to pick
> up the tab—even when she'd invited them. A male voice
> boomed out: "Sure thing, sweetheart."

Culture Counts: Establishing Relationships Abroad

Jessica, an automotive parts buyer, couldn't understand why her local Japanese supplier wouldn't accept her business proposal. He gave no indication of what the problem was. He just kept politely refusing her overtures. Jessica became increasingly frustrated, and finally called her predecessor, who had been promoted to another position in the company. Her predecessor listened and finally said, "When did you last see him?"

"See him?! Why, never," Jessica replied.

Immediately, her predecessor said, "That's the problem; you'll never do business with him until you meet him."

What Went Wrong?

In many cultures, you must establish a personal relationship before you can do business. Don't be impatient with this "getting-to-know-you" step; it builds trust. You may even spend a lot of time socializing, but again, it's a necessary part of establishing the needed relationship.

Some companies are realizing this: One financial consulting firm that I work with sent a number of employees to the Netherlands for a long weekend to meet their teammates since they would be working on a long-term project together and they wanted people to get to know one another.

Whether you are working internationally or in the United States, you will be interacting with people from other cultures. You can be on your best "American" behavior and still offend people as Jessica did, and not even know it!

Most of the blunders Americans make while doing business internationally can genuinely be attributed to ignorance, not malice. Regardless, the damage is often significant. Clients have been lost and negotiations have gone sour as a result.

16. Clues to communicating across cultures.

1. *Learn about other cultures.* The daily protocols of life and business vary not only in our companies, but from country to country (even on the same continent). If you understand those differences, you will be more successful when you work with people from other countries. When I ask participants in my global business etiquette seminar, "On what side of the street do the British drive?" many answer, "The wrong side!" It's not the wrong side, it's the *other* side. It's not usually a matter of right or wrong, it's a matter of differences. You want to know the differences.

   Don't be like Jessica; do your homework if you are interacting with people from other cultures. If your company provides training, take advantage of it, even if it's not part of your immediate job description.

   The Internet makes it very easy to learn about other cultures—just try googling "etiquette" and the name of the country or region; for example, "etiquette Germany," and you will find more information than you even need to know! A good website that has country-specific information on a number of countries is www.executiveplanet.com. And, of course, many culture-specific guidebooks are also available to tell you about the particular customs of a country.

Pachter's Pointer: You can't know everything about every culture . . .

But you can know the questions to ask about a culture, which are the same wherever you go in the world. It's just the answers that are different. Once you know the questions, figuring out the answers will be a lot easier.

2. *Recognize that it is the visitor who must adapt.* This is the standard rule of international etiquette: You are the visitor; you must adapt—otherwise, there would be chaos. On the other hand, it is a very gracious host who meets his or her visitors more than halfway. You will reap big dividends if you do.

3. *Do not react negatively to the differences you encounter.* Don't make negative comments about a custom you are unused to or feel uncomfortable with. Be respectful of the differences you encounter. You may find you enjoy dinner at 10 p.m. in Spain. If asked, I may say, "That's very different from what we experience in the United States." And don't make fun of other languages: Two Americans working for a Japanese firm in the United States were caught mimicking Japanese accents. They were fired.

Pachter's Pointer: It's just not nice.

It is just plain old-fashioned rudeness to negatively compare (or brag about) your culture and customs with those of another country or culture.

There are often cultural differences in the way people from varying cultures communicate nonverbally that can affect establishing connections. Among them are:

1. *Eye contact.* This is an area where many Americans abroad stumble. In the United States, you are encouraged to look

BLUNDER BUSTER

Learn to communicate in your discomfort zone. Mentally prepare for these differences so they won't interfere with your ability to listen and understand.

someone directly in the eye while speaking to that person, but in some Asian cultures, for example, you look away to show respect.

2. *Space.* In the United States, the average distance between two people talking with one another is approximately three feet. Yet you may find yourself talking to people who stand significantly closer to you, as in Latin America; and in other cultures, such as Japan, you will find people stand farther away.

3. *Gestures.* The meaning of a gesture can differ depending upon where in the world you are. The circle made by the thumb and index fingers with the remaining three fingers upright means "okay" in the United States; elsewhere it symbolizes something vulgar.

Learn the Lingo: Conversations Around the World

Simon, the director of a jewelry consortium, was seated in first-class returning to New York from the Middle East. He's a very tall, large man. Two men across from him were speaking French when Simon realized they were talking about him as "He's a brute." Simon speaks French fluently, so he leaned over and said in perfect French, "If you think I'm big, you should see my brother!"

What Went Wrong?

Always assume that the language you are speaking will be understood by those around you, so never say anything you wouldn't want anyone within earshot to hear.

17. If you don't speak the language . . .

If your counterpart speaks English, but you don't speak their language, here are some tips I picked up on my first job as a teacher of English as a second language

1. *Speak slower, not louder* when speaking to someone who is not a native speaker of English.

2. *Avoid idioms, jargon, and buzzwords.* They don't translate well across languages. Try explaining to someone what "all the bells and whistles on this job!" means. Duh!

Topics For Conversation

Do talk about: weather, climate, geography, films, art, sports, places of interest, your immediate surroundings, food.

Do not talk about: religion (though sincere questions about a religious practice can be okay), sex, politics. In some countries, such as France and Saudi Arabia, spirited debates are enjoyed, but when in doubt, avoid them.

---

3. *Avoid jokes and humor.* In general, humor doesn't translate well. I tell my clients, don't be humorous, but have a sense of humor—that's what's important.

 Pachter's Pointer: And speaking of foreign languages . . .

> Even if the person you're speaking with does speak English as a first language (for example, the English, Australians, and, yes, even the Canadians) you still need to be aware of differences in the meaning of words.

4. *Learn a few words* in the language of the country you are visiting; it will be noticed and usually appreciated.

5. *Use last names.* It's always better to be more formal at first than less. You can always be less formal, but it is more difficult if you are too informal too soon.

PART TWO

Dining, Drinking, and Other "Strictly Business" Social Occasions

What happens to otherwise professional people when they're away from the office and socializing for business? What makes them drink too much, dress inappropriately, tell tactless stories, and curse at the boss, the client, or a coworker? What makes them forget that they are the host? Does some wire in the brain short-circuit, causing them to make mistakes they would never in a million years make in the office?

No, that's not it. Amazing as it may seem, they forget (some may not know) that their behavior *outside* the office is just as important as their work *inside* the office. They simply don't get it: Business rules apply no matter what the setting—at restaurants, banquets, conferences, company picnics, boss's homes, or holiday celebrations.

The consequences that may arise from not understanding this simple rule can be enormous, ranging from losing business or a job, to stalling a career or losing the respect of your customer, client, colleague, employee, vendor, or boss. To make sure this nightmare doesn't happen to you, read on.

"Let's Do Lunch":
When You Are the Host

In her previous job, Sandra had been a successful account manager. She was now in a new position, in a new company, where much emphasis was placed on social interaction with customers. When she invited her first potential customer out for dinner, she was far from a success. She was unfamiliar with the restaurant—she'd chosen it because it was conveniently located—and, as it turned out, it was popular with the "happy hour" crowd and was quite noisy. To make matters worse, she and her customer were seated near a table of eight who were loudly celebrating a birthday. The service was poor; the food was mediocre. Sandra's knowledge of food and wine was limited and it showed. The evening was a flop. The account went to a competitor.

What Went Wrong?

Creating a comfortable and gracious atmosphere when entertaining signals your ability to put people at ease and take charge of situations—both important business skills. Your clients and customers want to work with people who are self-assured. When choosing between two equally competent people, they will almost always choose the one with better social graces.

BLUNDER BUSTER

Take action.

At the very least, when Sandra realized they were seated next to a large, noisy group, she should immediately have asked to be moved away from the revelers.

Had she arrived early and seen *and* heard the ruckus, she might have quickly called a nearby restaurant, then waylaid her guest with a line like, "They're having a party here tonight; I found a charming restaurant only a block away. I think you'll enjoy it better and we can talk quietly."

18. Six ways to make sure you are the host(ess) with the most(est)

1. *Pick a good restaurant.* You want a restaurant that is known for consistently good food and service. Though the new hot restaurant in town can be a good choice, make sure the ambience of the room lends itself to conversation. Ask knowledgeable friends and associates to make a recommendation, or purchase a reputable guide to restaurants in your town. If you're unsure about a restaurant's quality or ambience, visit without the guest first. Always make reservations. You don't want to arrive only to be turned away or faced with a long wait.

2. *Take nothing for granted.* Reconfirm your reservation. Arrive about fifteen minutes ahead of time. Check that your table is in a good location. You don't want to be near a service station or en route to the restrooms, and in some restaurants (especially in winter), you may not want to be close to the front

door. Greet your guest when he or she arrives and shake hands properly. Be prepared to make conversation.

3. *Make suggestions.* Comment on some of the menu items, such as, "They are famous for their lobster dumplings." You can recommend both appetizers and entrées. Suggest foods that are relatively easy to eat. You don't want your guest to have to wrestle escargot out of the shell. Your guest's order should be taken first. If your server wants to take your order first, defer to your guest by saying: "Joe, please order," or you can politely tell the waitperson, "Please take my guest's order first."

▶ **QUICK TIP:** Don't say: "Order anything; it's on my expense account." Instead of sounding gracious, which may be your intention, it will make you appear to be someone who takes advantage of others.

 ### Pachter's Pointer: Keep the table balanced.

This means do as your guest does. If your guest orders an appetizer, dessert, or a drink, you should, too (your drink doesn't have to contain alcohol). Your goal is to make your guest feel comfortable, and he might feel awkward if you have nothing while he eats or drinks.

4. *Pay attention.* Ask your guest if he needs anything, such as another drink, water, or more bread. It's your responsibility to signal the waiter. If a difficult situation arises, take charge.

5. *Make small talk.* Don't rush to talk about business. The best time to transition from non-business to business talk is after your food orders have been taken. If possible, wrap up the discussion before the food arrives. If not, talk about other things during the meal, and bring up business again over dessert.

6. *Say goodbye.* Escort your guest to the door. Retrieve his or her coat. Arrange for a taxicab or car service, if necessary. Thank your guest for coming and shake hands. As you are saying goodbye, refer to any follow-up to your discussion that will occur. "I'll get that proposal to you by the end of the week."

19. What about wine?

Mark, a rep for a toy company, took a customer to dinner at a fine French restaurant. He ordered a very expensive white wine. The customer put sugar and ice into the glass to sweeten and cool the wine. Mark now thinks carefully about where he takes this customer to dinner.

Although more and more people drink wine, it's still a mystery to many of us. It needn't be; it's really quite easy to learn a little about wine. There are many books and loads of information on the Internet. You also can take a class at a community college or local wine shop, if you want to learn more.

When selecting wine for your guests:

1. *Ask what your guest prefers.* If no preference is expressed and you are unsure about what to order, it's fine to ask the sommelier (wine steward) or waiter for suggestions.

   Although it is not carved in stone, you are usually safe ordering red wines with red meat; white wines with white meats or fish.

   • Popular reds: Shiraz, Zinfandel, and Pinot Noir

   • Popular whites: Chardonnay and Sauvignon Blanc

BLUNDER BUSTER

If you don't know a lot about wine, and if you know your guest is a connoisseur, it's fine to gracefully defer to him or her.

- Rosés are gaining popularity, especially in summer, but it's still safer to stay away from them unless your guest expresses an interest.

2. *One bottle for three people* is a good rule of thumb.

3. *When the wine is served:* The bottle will be shown to you to make sure it's what you ordered. Nod your approval.

- After the bottle is opened, inspect the cork. Do not sniff it. You want to be certain the cork is intact; that will demonstrate that air has not entered the bottle, which could spoil the taste.

- A small amount of wine will then be placed in your glass. You may sniff, taste a bit, or do both. Again, you want to make certain it has not spoiled. Nod your approval. Wine will then be poured into your guests' glasses; yours is filled last.

- Send wine back *only* if it is spoiled. Do not send the wine back because you do not like the taste.

"It's Not What You Eat . . .": When You Are the Guest

Joshua, an honor student and recently graduated chemical engineer, was being courted by a prominent company for the job of his dreams. He was unfamiliar with the city and had difficulty finding his way to the restaurant. As a result, he was late to arrive. When it was time for him to order, he chose the most expensive item on the menu. Served before the others, he immediately began to eat and—because he ate quickly—finished before the others were served. He did not get the job.

What Went Wrong?

Joshua, bright as he was, did not understand the importance of the business meal. True, he was probably nervous. True, he was in a strange environment. But it is also true that a dinner interview is a test, and it hadn't occurred to him that how he handled himself outside of the office would affect how others—in this case, his prospective employers—would view him.

Whether your dinner meeting is a job interview or if it is a meeting with a client, it is business and you must prepare for it as you would any other interview or business meeting.

20. Seven ways to succeed as a business guest.

In addition, bear these things in mind and you won't go wrong:

1. *Watch your Ps and Qs.* Be on your best behavior. You will be judged on it. Often people invite you to a business lunch so they can observe how you handle yourself outside of the office to determine whether they want to do business with you, promote you, or, as in Joshua's case, hire you.

   Sometimes the first interview is a business lunch. If you don't measure up, there may be no second interview. This may sound harsh, but often there are two or more equally talented people applying for a job or competing for an account. How is an employer or client going to decide who is better qualified? As Joshua learned the hard way, a business meal can be very revealing. I know a woman who didn't get a job offer because she "double-dipped" the guacamole. The head hunter told her that the VP took it as a sign she was either inconsiderate or thoughtless—qualities the VP felt disqualified her.

   Sometimes it's nothing that dramatic—often it just comes down to comfort level. Is the prospective employer or client comfortable with you? A meal is a good way to find out.

2. *Arrive on time.* Know where you are going and how to get there. Assume there will be traffic. If you are unfamiliar with the area, call ahead and ask the restaurant for directions or check a map service on the Internet.

3. *Dress for the occasion.* If you don't know what's appropriate, ask someone. If this isn't possible, think about the event, what you'll be doing, and who is going to be there, and remember it is always better to err on the more—rather than less—formal side.

4. *Make conversation.* Say something nice about the restaurant and continue making conversation during the meal.

5. *Mind your table manners.* If you are uncertain about the right way to use your utensils, ask someone to show you before you go. Many people hold their utensils incorrectly and don't realize it (see pages 57–59).

   • Do not chew with your mouth open or talk with your mouth full.

   • Don't pick your teeth. If something gets caught, go to the restroom.

   • Do not put your purse or briefcase on the table.

6. *Order a mid-priced dish,* unless your host recommends something more expensive. If your host doesn't make any recommendations, it's okay to ask for one.

7. *Write a thank-you note.* Use good stationery and mail the note within twenty-four hours.

And speaking of ordering . . .

Marty, a director at a large company, was asked by a neighbor to recommend his nephew, Jack, for a position at Marty's company. Marty liked Jack's résumé, but wanted to meet him before he decided to recommend him, so he invited him to lunch at a nearby restaurant. Marty ordered a salad. Jack ordered chicken fingers and fries, and proceeded to eat with his fingers. Needless to say, Marty didn't recommend Jack for a job.

1. *Order something that is easy to eat, that you like to eat, and that you know how to eat.* If you don't know how to eat some-

thing, don't order it. This is not the time to experiment. Avoid anything messy, including a large juicy hamburger, spaghetti, French onion soup, or lobster.

2. *Do not hold up the order because you can't decide.* You will come across as an indecisive person if you can't even decide what you want.

On the other hand,

3. *Use common sense.* If everybody orders lobster and makes a mess, it's fine to join them. Conversely, you don't want to be the only one with a bib on at a fancy restaurant when everyone in your party has ordered meat or chicken!

These days, it's not uncommon to find people with certain dietary restrictions, either for religious or health reasons or simple personal preference, which is why I recommend asking your guests before making reservations if they have any food preferences. If your dietary restrictions prevent you from eating certain foods and your host hasn't inquired, politely let him know ahead of time if you can. If that's not possible, don't make a fuss; simply order what you can. Most restaurants offer or can provide a vegetarian plate or request a large salad as your entrée.

▶ **QUICK TIP:** Eat a little something before you go out. This way, you won't be starving if the meal is delayed or it's not your favorite food. Remember, it's hard to be polite when you're ravenous.

Pachter Pointer: The purpose of a business meal is business, *not* food.

Though you do need to eat. The social atmosphere of a restaurant is meant to set the stage, to help the participants get to know one another. If you keep this is mind, dining out becomes much easier. Once you get the hang of it, you may discover that business lunches and dinners can be quite enjoyable as well as helpful to your career or business.

The "Secret" Language of Restaurant Dining

Phyllis took Paulo, her best customer, out to dinner at a very chic, very new, and very expensive restaurant. They decided what they were going to order, and continued to chat. After some time, the waiter had not returned to take their orders. Paulo was accustomed to getting what he wanted when he wanted it and eventually began to grumble. "Aren't we important enough for this restaurant? Do you have to be a movie star to get the waiter to take your order?" Phyllis looked down at the table and up at Paulo, and said, "I guess it may actually be our fault. We got so involved talking, we never closed the menus."

What Went Wrong?

Closing your menu tells the server that you have finished deciding and are ready to order. It's not hard to learn and once you learn the lingo, you'll feel less hassled and more comfortable in restaurants.

Similarly, when you have finished a course, the fork and knife should be placed diagonally across the plate, knife on top and fork below. (If the plate were a clock, the utensils would be at 10 and 4.) This nonverbal signal tells the waiter that you have finished eating and also makes it easier for the staff to remove your plate. Do *not* push your plate away from you or stack your plates when you have finished.

21. Decoding restaurant logic: the place setting and serving the meal.

1. *Know your place setting.* The following situation is not uncommon:

Sherry took her neighbor's bread. Frank, who was sitting next to her, unable to find his bread, asked, "Who took my bread?" Ultimately, everyone was talking about whose bread was whose and who it was that started the confusion, distracting everyone from the purpose of the lunch meeting, which was to plot strategy for the next sales conference.

Place settings vary depending on which restaurant you visit, but there are some standard guidelines that will help. Here are a few easy ways to keep track:

Food is placed to the *left* of the dinner plate. This memory

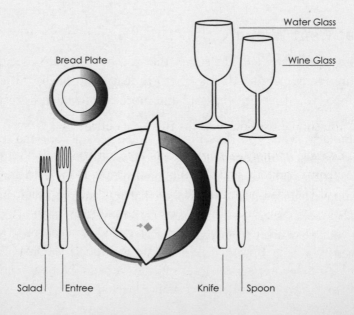

Water Glass

Bread Plate

Wine Glass

Salad   Entree   Knife   Spoon

BLUNDER BUSTER

If you have used the wrong utensil for a course, when the course arrives for which you need that utensil, just ask the waiter for another. If a dinner companion uses your utensil, quietly ask the server for another.

---

trick may help: The words *food* and *left* each have four letters; if the table is set properly, your bread or salad or any other *food* dish will be placed to the *left* of your dinner plate.

Similarly, drinks of any kind are placed to the *right* of the dinner plate, and the words *glass* and *right* contain five letters. Any *glass* or *drink* will be placed to the *right* of the dinner plate.

Voilà. You will no longer "steal" your neighbor's bread!

This memory trick also works for your utensils. Your fork (four letters) goes to the left; your knife and spoon (five letters each) go to the right.

The smaller fork is the salad fork; the larger is for the entrée. Each course should have its own utensils, and, as a rule, you should use your utensils from the outside in.

2. *Utensils are not weapons.* People notice if you don't hold your utensils correctly, and may think less of you. Don't hold the fork as if it were a pitchfork. Its handle should not be visible when you cut your food. Open your hand and place it inside your palm, so that it is leaning against your index finger. Bend your fingers in and position your thumb to support the fork. Turn your palm over and use your index finger and thumb to maneuver it. The knife is held in a similar fashion.

There are two ways to maneuver your knife and fork: American style and continental or European style. Both are correct, but you should be consistent and use one style or the other. (*Warning:* If you choose to use continental style in the United States, many people will look at you strangely. If you eat American style overseas, people may laugh at you.)

If you are right-handed, the fork goes in the left hand, and the knife in the right, for cutting. It's the reverse for lefties. Keep your elbows close to your sides when you cut your food. And do *cut* your food, don't *saw* at it!

Whichever style you choose, cutting your food is the same; how you use your utensils is another story:

- *American style:* After cutting your food, place the knife at the top of the plate (blade facing in) and switch your fork to your right hand and eat with your fork. Then pick up the knife and start again.

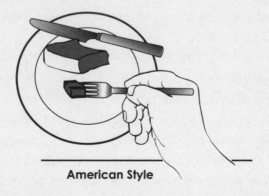

American Style

Pachter's Pointer: When eating American style . . .

You may cut up to three pieces of meat at a time. Yes, it is arbitrary, but in America if there aren't guidelines, some people might cut up everything on the plate! That would be very messy—and somewhat childlike. Not the impression you want to leave.

On the other hand, if you accidentally cut four pieces, don't worry about it. Chances are no one will notice.

- *Continental style:* Here, the fork stays in your left hand. You spear the meat, and, after cutting it, you may use the knife to push additional food onto the back of your fork, bringing your food to your mouth, fork tines down.

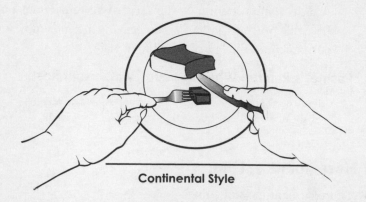

Continental Style

3. *Your napkin is* not *a washcloth.* Do not use your napkin to clean you face or as a Kleenex. Use it only to gently blot or pat at your mouth. And don't tuck your napkin into your shirt or belt!

Never use the tablecloth as a napkin! Yes, it happens. Someone in my seminar told this story about himself: At the time he was very young, new to the job, and didn't know his dinner companions very well. He was too shy to ask for a napkin, and instead, tucked the tablecloth into his pants. As he put it, "If I was too shy to ask for a napkin, can you imagine how embarrassed I was when I forgot what I had done and got up from the table?"

Napkin dos:

- When your host puts the napkin on her lap, it is the signal to put your napkin on yours. If there is no "official" host, put the napkin on your lap when you sit down. In some restaurants, your server may help you with your napkin.

- Place the fold of the napkin facing your waist. It is less likely to fall off.

- Place your napkin on your chair if you temporarily leave the table. In some restaurants, the server will refold your napkin while you are gone. When leaving permanently, put your napkin to the left of the dinner plate.

 Pachter's Pointer: When in doubt, watch your host.

If you don't know what to do, watch your host and do what he or she does. You may not be right, but you're not wrong!

22. More about eating.

- Sit up straight, no slouching.

- Tear your bread; butter one piece at a time.

- Move your soup spoon away from you in the bowl, lift it, and then bring it back to your mouth. A student used this rhyme to remember the rule: *As my ship goes out to sea, I move my spoon away from thee.*

- Pass food to the right.

- If something isn't right, don't make a fuss; try to ignore it or unobtrusively ask for what you need.

Slurping Your Soup and Other Dining Don'ts

Two CPAs from the same company were in the running for a promotion. The boss took Lucy and Nora out to dinner. When Henry, her future boss, told Lucy she was chosen, she asked what had set her apart. He said, "Nora added salt to her food before she tasted it." Although it was a small thing, Henry took it as an indication of rash behavior.

What Went Wrong?

Do not season your food before tasting it. Many people think doing this indicates that the person makes assumptions before having all the facts or take it, as Henry did, as an indication of rashness. Henry may not have been correct in his analysis, but the candidates were equally qualified and he had to base a decision on something.

Everything we do at work can have consequences. Good manners dictate tasting your food before adding seasoning to it in any situation, business or social. There is one interesting exception to this rule—pepper. Because pepper quickly loses its aroma and flavor, many restaurants offer to add pepper to your food, especially to salads, before you've had a chance to taste it.

▶ **QUICK TIP:** Adding ketchup to your food is generally considered an insult to the chef. But what about French fries? I was recently asked, "Is it better to pour the ketchup on the fries or to puddle and dip?" (I get asked some very creative questions!) If you want to add ketchup, then puddle and dip; it's less messy. And use your fork to cut the fries into bite-size pieces. If you use your fingers, it's too messy, with or without ketchup.

23. Eight dining don'ts.

1. Don't *groom yourself at the table.* No washing. No reapplying makeup (yes, not even lipstick!). No hair combing, either. Go to the restroom.

2. Don't *ask to share food at a business meal.* And do not take food off someone else's plate. Sharing among families and friends is not uncommon in the United States, but it's a definite no-no for business meals. One team I coached complained about their supervisor, who helps herself from their plates whenever she takes them out to lunch. She "just wants a taste . . . ," but she doesn't even ask permission! You can't blame them for not wanting to go out with her.

3. Don't *make noise when you eat,* unless you are in Japan, where it can be a sign of appreciation for the food (see the next section for more information on international dining.)

4. Don't *smoke* unless your host or guest does. It goes without saying, smoke only if the restaurant has a smoking section.

5. Don't *yell or behave badly to the servers.* If there is a problem, talk to the person in private and explain the problem.

6. Don't *take or make phone calls.* Turn your cell phone *off.* That means completely off. Some people think they can set their phone to vibrate and sneak a peek to find out who is calling; that's not good enough. Unless your wife is expecting a baby

(in which case you should mention that fact to your companion), there are few calls that can't wait until after the meal.

7. Don't *point out other people's mistakes*. It can be embarrassing.

8. Don't *ask for a doggy bag*.

Closing the Culture Gap: Dining Internationally

Nathan, a sales rep, wanted to show a customer from India visiting the United States for the first time some typical American activities. He thought the man would enjoy visiting his home for a "typical American barbeque," where he served hot dogs and hamburgers. The customer ate very little, became rather aloof, and left early.

What Went Wrong?

Nathan graciously invited the customer to his home; unfortunately, the customer was a vegetarian. Nathan should have looked into Indian culture to see if there might be dietary issues. If he had, he would have learned that many Indians are Hindu and some are vegetarians; others will eat no beef because the cow is sacred in India; still others are Muslim and will eat no pork.

He should also have asked the man about dietary requirements. As we've discussed, you should do this for any guest, but it's especially important when you are entertaining visitors from other countries.

Still, the Indian man was a guest in Nathan's home and, therefore, he should have chalked it up to Nathan's unfamiliarity with Hindu dietary restrictions instead of thinking Nathan was deliberately behaving rudely. Had he done so, he might not have reacted negatively.

24. When you are a guest in foreign lands . . .

1. Don't *refuse food.* Accepting food and drink demonstrates acceptance of your host. People too often say, "I can't eat that!" But try a little bit. You may surprise yourself and like it. Besides, there really isn't any polite way to refuse food unless you are truly allergic or there is a religious or dietary prohibition against eating it. If you lie and it is discovered, you can destroy your host's trust. Something you might try, which works for me, is to swallow quickly and don't ask what it is! In Holland I ate raw herring because it was a local specialty even though I don't care for raw food.

▶ **QUICK TIP:** When in China, leave a little on your plate. The U.S. custom of leaving a clean plate has a different meaning in China, where your host may perceive it as an indication that you weren't served enough food.

2. Don't *talk negatively about the different dining customs* you encounter. In an Austrian restaurant, I sat next to another diner and his dog. Dogs are quite common in Parisian restaurants as well. While this story told to me by one of my students doesn't quite fall into the category of a dining custom, it does illustrate differences in customs: In Taiwan she dined one evening with her host's wife and the next night with his mistress.

3. Do *use utensils correctly.* Hold your utensils properly. Know the difference between the American and continental use of the knife and fork (see pages 57–59). In some cultures, be prepared to eat with chopsticks or your fingers. In others, such as Saudi Arabia, it's improper to eat with your left hand; it's considered the "dirty" hand. In fact, even offering something to someone with your left hand can be considered rude.

"I'll Get This": Who Pays?

Marnie, a director of sales, invited her administrative assistant, Joanne, to lunch at an expensive restaurant to talk about plans for an upcoming conference. When the check arrived, Marnie asked Joanne to split the bill. Needless to say, Joanne was really upset.

What Went Wrong?

Marnie should have paid. Since she invited Joanne, she was the host, and, therefore, she should have paid the bill. Many companies have a policy that the person with the highest rank picks up the tab. Since Marnie was the highest-ranking person, she should have paid.

25. No muss, no fuss: The discreet art of paying checks.

1. *Do it behind the scenes.* Have the maître d' or your server imprint your credit card ahead of time. At the end of the meal, excuse yourself and sign the check or tell the restaurant when you arrive to add the gratuity and hand you the receipt as you leave. It's much more elegant if the check does not come to the table.

2. *Use a credit card.* When paying at the table, this is especially useful. It's quicker and easier to leave a tip and you will have a record of the expense.

3. *Tip appropriately.* The rule of thumb is 15 to 20 percent before tax. Some U.S. restaurants will add the gratuity to the

check for large parties. Internationally, the tip will often be included in the check, although in some countries if the service is especially good, you should consider adding a small additional gratuity. It's a good idea to check into the proper custom before you leave on an international business trip.

Pachter's Pointer: For women only . . .

When you host a man who wants to pick up the check, you have some choices:

1. Pay the bill behind the scenes, or

2. If the bill comes to the table, say, "It's not me; my company is paying for this."

If the man *still* insists, let him. You don't want to ruin a good business relationship over a bill.

4. *Don't make a scene.* If, for example, the bill is incorrect, speak to the waiter privately. If is not resolved, and it's a major issue, excuse yourself and talk to the manager privately. The point is that you don't want to embarrass your guest.

Rules of the Buffet Table

1. No butting into the line.

2. Wait your turn.

3. Talk to the people around you, but don't complain about the length of the line or the quality of the food.

4. Use the serving utensils.

5. Don't overfill your plate or take numerous plates at one time.

6. Make as many trips you wish to the buffet line, as long as it's not so often it is noticed.

7. Eat foods in their "traditional" order; no matter how great a chocoholic you are, don't start with a hot fudge sundae!

8. Don't make sarcastic remarks or get nasty if the buffet runs out of your favorite dish.

9. Don't take food from the serving plate and put it directly into your mouth; put it on your plate first.

"Oh, My Gosh!": Irresponsible Drinking

Marissa, a production supervisor at a printing plant, drank too much at the retirement party of someone on her staff. Marissa's boss, Frank, also attended the party and when Marissa saw him, she began yelling and cursing at him about a new policy he had initiated. She was fired on the spot. When she arrived for work the next day, she couldn't understand why her ID card didn't open the security gate. She had no memory of anything that had happened the night before!

What Went Wrong?

You will encounter alcohol in many business situations. How you drink (including how much you drink) and hold your liquor (that is, whether you honestly know your limit—and it's different for all of us) tells others a lot about you. Even if you say you are one of those folks who never gets drunk and never says or does anything inappropriate if you do, a business setting is not the place to let your hair down. It makes you appear unprofessional and just sends the wrong message all the way around. With a little discipline, you'll wake up without a hangover and—unlike our production supervisor—with a job.

26. How to avoid the "morning-after" blues.

1. *Never get drunk.* "Bottoms-up!" is not a corporate slogan. Careers have been stalled and jobs have been lost because

people got drunk and said and did ridiculous—sometimes self-destructive, as in the example above—things. Business social events are meant to be fun, but don't forget your behavior *always* counts.

2. *Set a limit for yourself.* For most of us, that limit is just one drink because after the first drink, it is all too easy to have the second, and, after the second, it is incredibly easy to have the third. And after the third, who cares! During a cocktail reception for a group of candidates for post-doctorate positions at a university, one applicant threw his arms around an assistant dean and slurred, "I love you, man." You know this was not the image the university wished to convey. You can bet the young post-doc cared when he didn't get the position, but it was too late.

3. *Drink creatively.* If you usually have scotch on the rocks, drink scotch and water. I know someone who took no chances. He arranged a signal with the bartender at a bar near his office: If he ordered gin and tonic, the bartender served him tonic on the rocks. If he ordered scotch and water, he got the liquor. When he was with clients, he usually ordered gin and tonic.

▶ **QUICK TIP:** To limit your drinking, one VP suggests ordering a drink that you don't like. He does it and says it allows him to nurse the one drink all night.

4. *Order a nonalcoholic beverage.* It's okay not to drink. Many people don't. But you do need to participate. Don't make a big deal of it or draw attention to the fact that you are not drinking; just order tomato juice, sparkling water, or a soft drink. If someone asks, you can say something like, "I have an early meeting tomorrow," or "I'm the designated driver."

When in Rome, or Russia, or Romania, Drink Wisely

My collaborator's husband often traveled to Russia to meet with scientists about publishing their books in English. Earl's not a big drinker, but, as he tells it, everywhere he went from ten in the morning on, just as we'd have a coffee break, they had a vodka or brandy break. He felt he was being rude to refuse their hospitality, so would take what they offered and drink a small amount—slowly.

One evening, he and a colleague were taking Yuri, an important physicist, to dinner at a very expensive restaurant in Moscow. They'd been trying for years to convince him to write a book especially for them. The vodka and wine were flowing, but Earl remembers nothing of their dinner until through the fog he heard himself saying, "Nyet!" to what he thought would be another drink. He then heard his colleague say, "But Earl, why shouldn't Yuri publish his book with us?" At that moment—and for the rest of the dinner—Earl stayed wide awake.

What Went Wrong?

Drinking too much can have negative consequences no matter where in the world you are. But in many European countries you may be encouraged to drink more than you otherwise would. Conversely, there are countries in the Middle East where religious beliefs prohibit any drinking. It is very important to know the rules before you go, and, wherever you go, if you do drink alcohol, be smart about how much you can handle. Otherwise, like Earl, you may truly find yourself with your foot in your mouth!

A Word to the Wise: The Rules Apply to the Family

A woman's husband drank too much at her company's holiday party. During the evening, as the president made his annual speech telling employees how grateful he was for their hard work, a voice from the back of the room bellowed, "If everyone is so wonderful, why do you pay them so little?" He did it three times!

Nothing was said, but the woman was laid off a week later.

---

27. How to drink without getting drunk (wherever you may be).

1. *Eat before you drink.* The liquor will affect you less with food in your stomach.

2. *Dilute your drink.* If you usually drink scotch on the rocks, drink scotch and water. It's less potent that way.

3. *Take small sips.* Your drink will last longer that way.

4. *Say "fill it up now."* If someone says, "Finish your drink, so I can refill it," politely say, "Oh, you can fill it up now."

5. *Be creative.* Find unusual ways to drink without really drinking: One man poured his drinks into the flowerpots that were scattered all round the room, which allowed him to "drink without getting drunk." If you do this, make sure that your host isn't looking!

Make the Most of the Moment: Mingling with Style and Grace

A group of pharmaceutical representatives invited physicians (their customers) to a dinner program at a fabulous hotel. The highlight of the evening was the keynote speaker—a well-known scientist discussing a hot topic of interest to all. There was no prearranged seating and many of the reps sat together. They also made no effort to mingle with their guests either before dinner or at the reception after the presentation. They stayed in their own group and talked among themselves. Their clients were bewildered; their district manager was furious.

What Went Wrong?

The representatives not only insulted their guests, but they also missed a key opportunity to get to know their customers better. All the goodwill that the company might have gained from the event was squandered.

It's a truism that people prefer to do business with people they know, like, and respect. Mingling at business social events allows you to get to know those you work with—not only clients, but colleagues and vendors—and have them get to know you outside of the traditional office setting. Its value can't be underestimated.

28. Eight ways to become a mingling maven.

Many people experience some form of nervousness in social situations. Business social situations are the bane of others, sometimes even to those who under other circumstances have no qualms about wading into a crowd. As with most things, the more experience you have, the easier it will be to score points in even the toughest business social situations.

1. *Practice.* Put yourself in situations where you must socialize. This means you have to attend events regularly.

 Pachter's Pointer: Challenge yourself.

Reach beyond your comfort zone and set a mingling goal. Your goal could be to attend at least one social event a month, or to meet a certain number of new people each week, or to make certain you say hello to a specific person. Keep your goals realistic and simple. Keep a record and monitor your progress.

2. *Be positive.* If you go to an event thinking you will have a horrible time, you will have a horrible time. If you go thinking, *I can mingle, this will be interesting, I'll have a good time,* you are much more likely to have a positive experience.

3. *Watch your body language.* Make sure it expresses a relaxed, open attitude. At business social events, many of us are nervous and freeze up, and our negative body language gives us away. Some people sport stern facial expressions; others cross their arms as if to ward off anyone who approaches. Some wring their hands, slump against the wall, or bite their nails—body language that screams "Stay away!"

It may at first be difficult, but force yourself to smile and relax your facial expression. Keep your hands at your sides and your body away from the wall. If you don't look or act nervous, people won't know you are nervous.

4. *Introduce yourself.* It's easier to mingle only with people you know, but this is business and your goal is also to meet new people. It's generally easier to approach someone who is also alone. Groups of two are often in private conversation and may not want to be disturbed, but the single person is often eager for the company. Simply say hello, introduce yourself, and shake hands.

5. *Join groups of three or more.* As you continue to mingle, challenge yourself to approach larger groups of people; you'll interact with more people and the burden to make conversation will be eased. Simply approach the group, listen for a while, and, when appropriate, introduce your comments by saying something like, "Something similar happened in our department . . ." You may also need to introduce yourself: "I'm Jane Scott, by the way. My company is one of this evening's sponsors."

6. *Vary your conversation.* Just because it's a business event doesn't mean you should only discuss business. A business social event is also supposed to be social, so lace your conversation with topics unrelated to work. If spouses or partners attend, it's even more important to make sure that you talk about things that will interest them as well. That means put a hold on shop talk and talk about things everyone has in common. Saying something about the event is always a good place to start, commenting on the speaker or that day's topic works well, too; even the weather is a fine ice-breaker.

7. *Ask questions.* Questions are a great way to encourage someone to talk. Responses such as the four that follow will help you continue the conversation.

   • *Expanding:* "Tell me more; it sounds as if you had a great time."

- *Comparing:* "That sounds similar to . . ."

- *Self-revealing:* "I know what you mean; I was in a similar situation last year."

- *Clarifying:* "What exactly did he do?"

8. *End the conversation graciously.* Exit talking. I don't mean you should let your voice trail off as you move farther and farther away. I do mean that you should respond to what the person was saying, or add a comment, and then close with an exit line. Good exit lines include:

- "It was great meeting you!"

- "Excuse me. I need to grab Christopher before he leaves."

- "Let's talk about this again soon." (Use this line only if you mean to follow up on it.)

- "I need to get going. I'll see you next week at the meeting."

If the other person is talking, and you only respond with an exit line, something like, "Nice talking to you," and then move off, it may seem that you weren't listening, which is rude. When you are talking, you can make the transition in a smooth, fluid manner.

I am always amazed at the lengths to which people go to end a conversation. In the strange but true category, I recently heard this story: Caroline, a new manager, was talking to Josie, a manager in another department who she had recently met. Josie, it seems, likes to tell stories—lots and lots of stories—and Caroline didn't have the time for a long chat. Finding it hard to end the conversation gracefully, Caroline tried walking into the restroom. Josie not only followed, but stood there waiting! Caroline really needed to use an exit line.

"Is This Really Necessary?": A Party at Your Boss's Home

Maria didn't enjoy socializing with her coworkers outside of the office. She made it a rule not to attend any out-of-the-office functions—not the company picnic, not the holiday party, not the baby or wedding shower—not a one. She told a friend, "I see these people all the time. Why do I have to socialize with them on my time?" One time her boss invited the entire department to his home as a thank-you for all their extra work on a major proposal. Almost everyone came, but again Maria was a no-show. At the party, Danielle spent some time talking to the new VP, the boss's boss, who unexpectedly stopped by. When Danielle received the next promotion Maria was surprised; she'd assumed it would be hers.

What Went Wrong?

Even though it's not in the office, an invitation to the boss's home is a business event. Your attendance and how you act matters. I promise you, not going will be noticed—and not in a positive manner. Not showing up sends a negative message to bosses as well as peers or customers. Going says you are a team player, and, as they say, greases the wheels by giving you an opportunity to get to know people in a less formal setting, establish and cement relationships that can affect your working relationships inside the office, and provide opportunities for networking.

BLUNDER BUSTER

If you are *really* (and I do mean really) unable to attend, let your host and other invitees know why. And your excuse better be good. Remember, you can only use your great-aunt Mildred's death once!

29. What to do when you are invited.

1. Do *attend*. Attendance is *not* optional. You need to make an appearance or have a very good reason not to. The same applies to your spouse or partner, if he or she is invited. One VP was told he was going no further in the company until his spouse or partner started attending company functions. And yes, it is important to arrive on time.

2. Do *RSVP*. If asked to RSVP, do so. It's difficult to plan an event—large or small—when you don't know how many people are coming.

3. Do *dress appropriately*. You want to look professional, even when the occasion is social and casual. (See Part Three for more about how to dress.)

4. Do *mingle*. Do not talk only to the people you know or know well. This is an opportunity to get to know others. (And as mentioned before, don't have too much to drink.)

5. Do *prep your spouse or partner*. Before the event, fill your spouse or partner in on who is going to be there, what your

connection with the other guests is, and any news about your work or department that might come up.

6. Do *send a thank-you note.* A handwritten note sent to the host's home is more personal than email. And don't forget to thank your boss's spouse or partner. Use nice stationery; that is, good-quality paper, ideally imprinted with your name. It is usually appropriate to bring a small gift, such as chocolates, candies, or cocktail napkins. And in some situations sending flowers the morning of the event or the day after can be a very gracious thank-you.

And by the way . . .

7. Do not *bring your pet!* To some of you, this may sound like a crazy piece of advice, but believe me, it happens. A manager who works for a Fortune 100 company invited his sales representatives to his home for an evening of team building. One of the reps thought it would be okay, even fun, to bring her dog to the party. She thought very wrong. Bringing her dog was bad enough, but the dog peed on the dining room rug. It took professionals to get the smell out of the rug, and the rep is still trying to win back her manager's respect.

I know that animals play a very important part in many people's lives, but unless you work for a company that allows pets or you have a disability and use a guide dog, keep your pet at home.

And while we're on the subject . . .

Company picnics, holiday parties, and other out-of-the-office diversions don't mean you can relax—at least not completely. To illustrate my point, let me tell you about a young man just beginning his

Thank-You Notes

You should send a note after visiting someone's home, being treated to a lunch, given a present, or after a job interview. If people go out of their way to help you, a note may also be warranted; it certainly is a nice gesture.

Not only is sending a note the right thing to do, it makes you stand out as a polished professional. Whom would you rather do business with—the person who acknowledges you or your effort or the one who doesn't?

A young man asked me if it was appropriate for a man to send another man a thank-you note. Emphatically, *yes*.

1. *Thank-you note vs. thank-you letter.* A thank-you note is a short, three- to four-sentence handwritten note. If your thank-you involves a number of paragraphs, which can happen after a plant tour or a job interview, you may want to type the letter to make it easier for people to read.

2. *Better late than never.* It's customary to send thank-yous within twenty-four hours, but if you don't do it within that time frame, do it anyway. Some may say, "Oh, it's too late to send one now." I say, "Do it anyway."

Sample thank-you notes:

Dear Tom,
   Thank you for hosting our department at your home. It was fun to get together with the team outside of the office. I had a great time and I know others did as well.
   Regards,

Dear Mr. Parker,
   Thank you for a lovely lunch. The restaurant was a great choice, the food was excellent and the conversation was stimulating. I look forward to speaking with you further about how our companies can work together.
   Thanks again.
   Sincerely,

BLUNDER BUSTER

Make it right.

If you accidentally break a dish, spill red wine on the tablecloth, or in any way damage something at your boss's (or for that matter, anyone's) home, apologize immediately, and do something to correct the mistake right away. If possible, send a replacement with a note apologizing or offer to pay the cleaning bill. One woman's boyfriend, admiring a set of candlesticks at her boss's house, picked one up; a spark flew, burning the tablecloth. They both immediately apologized. The next day, the woman sent the boss and his spouse a note along with a gift card to a linen store.

---

career: The day was glorious, the pool inviting. It was Norm's first visit to his boss's home—a summer party—and all was going well. Whatever possessed him to take a cannonball dive into the swimming pool we'll never know. We do know that water splashed everywhere and everyone. We also know that neither Norm's boss nor his wife thought it was funny.

Once you enter the business world, it's time to grow up! Teenage activities and pranks probably weren't all that funny when you were a kid, and they're definitely not funny now. Juvenile behavior will make you look foolish and detract from your credibility, even at an informal, fun event like a swim party. So, it pays to remember these two simple rules:

1. Your behavior *always* matters.

2. Remember that in business social situations, business rules apply.

Pachter's Pointer: Things not to do at a corporate function.

But, sad to say, they have all been done in the workplace:

- go home with the boss's son or daughter
- bring your current fling (if you are married) to a company holiday party
- put a whoopee cushion on a colleague's seat

Entertaining at Your Home

Every year around the holidays Tom invited his staff to his home for a Friday-night dinner to celebrate. This was a gracious and welcome act and his staff was always pleased. At one such event, Tom's wife was out of town. Shortly after the meal was served, Tom excused himself and left the table to put his three-year-old son to bed. He was gone for at least twenty minutes. This made his guests uncomfortable; should they continue to eat or wait for him to return?

What Went Wrong?

If done well, entertaining at home can add a lot to your professional image. It sends the message that you are a boss who appreciates his or her team; one who will go the extra mile for his or her staff. It tells clients that you are grateful for their business and don't take them for granted. At the same time, common blunders can detract from your image and even undermine your authority.

30. Ten tips for successful entertaining at home.

1. *Provide the necessary information.* Your employees need to know if spouses or partners or dates are invited, the dress code, the time the party starts and ends, and whether or not a meal will be served.

2. *Check dietary requirements.* Many people are vegetarians or have restrictions. If you don't know your guests' requirements, ask before you plan the menu. Make sure there is something

everyone can eat. Keep the food simple and easy to eat. Forget about spareribs or spaghetti.

3. *Prepare your spouse or partner.* Let your spouse or partner know who is coming and why. Try to share something about each person so that your spouse or partner can make conversation with all of your guests.

4. *Prepare your children.* If they are old enough to understand, explain what is happening and what their role, if any, is. If your children are young, hire a babysitter to look after them. You don't want them distracting your guests.

▶ **QUICK TIP:** If you have pets, keep them away from guests. Some people are frightened of dogs; others may dislike cats; still others are allergic to animals.

5. *Clean your* entire *house.* You don't want to undermine your image with a dirty bathroom or a messy home office.

6. *Keep an eye on liquor consumption.* When you serve alcoholic beverages of any kind, it is your responsibility to make sure that no one gets drunk, and that includes you! Offering only wine and beer rather than hard liquor is simpler and safer, but even with these, many people can become drunk. As the host, be alert, and, if someone does overdo it, make sure he or she doesn't drive home drunk.

7. *Mingle with everyone.* Help others mingle, too. If your guests don't all know one another, make the introductions.

8. *Get help serving and cleaning up.* If the budget will allow, you'll find that this is money well spent. It will free you up to interact with your guests.

9. *Choose music that everyone will like* and that won't interfere with conversation. Hard rock blaring from speakers in every room makes it impossible to talk with the person standing next to you. Jazz or classical music is often a good choice. Whatever you choose, play it softly in the background so people can speak comfortably.

10. *Say a few words to welcome your guests* and let them know you appreciate their efforts or, if you are entertaining clients, their business.

Gifts, Glorious Gifts: Where to Draw the Line

A director for a public relations firm received a lace teddy as a gift from a vendor at a surprise birthday party for her. She opened her gifts in front of everyone. Many people gave her lighthearted gifts, like coffee mugs and T-shirts with clever sayings. When she opened the package with the teddy, she blushed a little, but said nothing. The vendor never got another order from her.

What Went Wrong?

It's work, not romance! It's hard to believe I need to say this, but based on experience I must. Do not give sexually suggestive gifts to a business associate. Even if you happen to share a copier by day and a bedroom at night, save the sexy gifts for private moments, far from the office. At work, it's best to avoid giving any gift that's too personal.

"Safe" gifts include neutral items such as books, CDs or DVDs, pens, plants, stationery, food or candy, homemade baked goods, small electrical gadgets, gift cards to a store, and/or tickets to a show or sporting event. Tailor them to the person's interests if you can. They may not be as eye-catching as lingerie, but that's the point!

Also spend an appropriate amount. What that is will depend on your position and the occasion. A general guideline for a work present is $10 to $100. But I do know of one extravagant boss who had a very successful year and bought his office manager a Rolex!

31. Guidelines for giving and receiving.

1. *Follow company guidelines.* Many companies have policies on what their employees may receive from vendors, customers, and clients. Follow them. Do not put someone in the embarrassing position of having to return a gift.

2. *Employees don't usually give bosses gifts.* It can look like culling favor. However, in some offices, usually smaller ones, everybody exchanges gifts for birthdays and/or the holidays.

3. *Contribute to the office gift pool.* Generally, contributing to the pool allows the recipient to get a bigger gift and saves most givers money. Taking part also makes you look like a team player. If you are close to the person and plan to give a personal gift, say that you will be doing it privately and therefore won't be contributing to a group gift.

   If you work in a large company and pools are more than you can comfortably afford, suggest that contributions to the pool be anonymous and that the amount of the contribution be at the giver's discretion (each person puts whatever amount he or she is comfortable with into an envelope and everyone signs the card). If it's a luncheon or dinner where the amount is specified, attend those where you work closely with the person whose event is being celebrated and politely decline to participate in those where you have little or no interaction. But be sure to attend some of the time. Consider suggesting a monthly pool for goodies to celebrate all the June birthdays.

4. *Send a card.* If a gift is not appropriate, it's almost always okay to send a card acknowledging an occasion. Make sure you sign the card and add a short handwritten note.

International Guide to Gift Giving

Accepting a gift: Customs vary from place to place. In China and other cultures, a gift must be declined before it is accepted. In other countries, such as Spain, a gift is opened immediately in front of the person who gave you the gift.

Wrapping a gift: In some cultures, especially the Japanese, the way a gift is wrapped is very important. To play it safe, let a store or hotel gift-wrap the item for you.

Choosing a gift: Food, candy, or a souvenir indigenous to your country or region is generally a good choice. So, too, is something that highlights the interests of the person to whom you are giving the gift. An illustrated book about the city you represent, calendars, pens, small electronic gifts, a framed photo taken during your trip are good options. Toys if the person has children. Liquor if allowed in the country. When I was leaving Abu Dhabi, my client offered me the choice of a good pen and pencil set or an electronic calendar.

Flowers: While flowers are often a good choice, before giving them, check out the local customs. Certain flowers or colors have different meanings in different countries; for example, in Germany, red roses are for lovers *only*; in Mexico, yellow flowers symbolize death.

PART THREE

A Professional Presence:
It's More Than *What* You Do,
It's *How* You Do It

D o you know what image you project when you walk
into a room, attend a meeting, visit a colleague, or
meet with a client or customer? Do you know what others
see? Most of us do not. Fact is, just as you project an image, others perceive what you are projecting. You have no
control over what others see. You control only what you
project.

To a large degree, your image is projected through verbal and nonverbal communication, including your dress,
which is a form of nonverbal communication. (In Part One,
we saw how establishing rapport and making connections
contribute to your professional image.) Yet, as important as

image is to professional success, it is astonishing how many people are unaware of how others *see* and *hear* them.

As with everything else in business (and in life), you will discover that there are right and wrong (or, at least, correct and incorrect) ways of doing things. As you become more and more aware of the image you project, you'll also discover ways to modify that image, to control what you project to colleagues, clients, customers, and coworkers—those who rank both higher and lower on the corporate ladder. An added reward is that these lessons also will serve you well in your interactions with friends and family.

Test Yourself: What Message Are You Sending?

	TRUE	FALSE
1. If I am comfortable with my arms crossed, it is okay to sit or stand that way when I am with a customer.	☐	☐
2. Occasional filler words such as "okay," "all right," "you know," "uh-huh" are always noticed.	☐	☐
3. In an informal situation with clients, it is okay to chew gum.	☐	☐
4. Visible body piercings are okay in most corporate settings.	☐	☐
5. Use the phrase "I'll be honest with you" to let people know you are telling the truth.	☐	☐
6. No more than one ring per hand and one bracelet per arm is the jewelry guideline for business.	☐	☐

	TRUE	FALSE
7. It is okay for women to wear sexy clothing to company social activities.	☐	☐
8. Slacks and polo shirts are acceptable casual clothes for men.	☐	☐

All the answers are false, except for numbers 6 and 8—they are true. Even if you answered all of the questions correctly, read on. You'll not only find out why these seemingly little things are so important, but you'll also pick up handy tips and techniques that will help you fine-tune your image.

LOOK THE PART: COMMUNICATE YOUR IMAGE—WORDLESSLY

Your Clothes Talk: What Message Do They Send?

On the first day of a two-day seminar at an off-site meeting, Grant, an excellent instructor of product safety, arrived dressed in professional casual attire—slacks and a sweater; on the second day, he sported an old sweatshirt and jeans. In evaluating the seminar, one participant wrote, "It just wasn't the same the second day. The seminar leader didn't seem in control and didn't hold our attention."

What Went Wrong?

While the participant couldn't put his finger on what went wrong, it's fairly obvious that the way Grant was dressed changed his audience's perception of him. He was not dressed appropriately for the situation. Even though the attendees now knew him, it was still important that he look like the instructor. His very casual appearance resulted in a loss of credibility. He simply didn't look the part.

Jennifer, the arts director for a community-wide arts center was sitting atop a ladder in overalls, paint smudges on her face, hair tied back in a ponytail, when an important donor arrived unexpectedly for an appointment that the owner believed had been scheduled for the following week. She was stunned; she looked at the donor, looked

BLUNDER BUSTER

Grant should have known better, and there was nothing he could do to remedy the situation. (He sensed a change but couldn't figure out why it was happening until he read the evaluations.) He can learn from the blunder and make sure that he doesn't make the same mistake again. Jennifer, on the other hand, made a quick and classy recovery.

at herself, and immediately said, "We're changing shows this week. Look at me! Give me five minutes to freshen up and I'll show you the canvases in the back room, and then I'll take you to lunch and we can talk."

32. What you wear *always* matters.

Your clothing represents you and it can enhance your professional image and your ability to be taken seriously or it can take away from it.

1. *Give your wardrobe a reality check.*
   Ask yourself, Are my clothes appropriate for:

   - my job?

   - the type of company that I work for?

   - my company's dress-code policy?

   - the event or activity?

   - the region of the country or the world that I am in?

What's appropriate for a business meeting is very different from what's appropriate for the company picnic. What's appropriate for a large corporate setting may be very different from what's right in a small office environment. What's appropriate for certain industries—Wall Street or pharmaceuticals, for example—may be very different from what's acceptable in the public relations or entertainment industries. In the United States, dress codes even vary in different parts of the country, and, if you travel internationally, keep in mind that what's appropriate for a business meeting in one country may be very different than what's appropriate in another.

2. *Check your calendar each evening.* Make certain you know what you are doing the following day and dress accordingly. An accountant I know wears business casual clothes when he's working in his office, which is small and casual, but when he visits clients' offices, he wears a suit. They expect him to look like a pro, and he doesn't want to let them down.

 Pachter's Pointer: Don't be caught off guard.

Keep a well-pressed jacket in a solid, dark color on a hanger in your office. Adding a jacket to whatever you are wearing upgrades most outfits. This is true for both men's and women's attire.

Consider keeping a pair of good, well-shined shoes (heels are usually best for women) in the office as well. Here, too, a dark color that will go with anything is a good choice.

Clothing Means Business: Business and Business Casual

Joan-Ellen interviewed for a job in a large corporate office groomed and dressed professionally in a business suit. Her first day on the job, she arrived in a short leather skirt, T-shirt-like top, fishnet stockings, and three-inch heels. She was told to go home and change, and warned in no uncertain terms that if she ever showed up that casual again she would be fired.

What Went Wrong?

Her clothes did not say "work," they screamed "party!" Between the interview and her first day on the job, Joan-Ellen had changed the type of clothing she was wearing and her new employers didn't like it one bit. They felt tricked—she no longer appeared to be the professional they had hired.

33. "Dress for success" is not just a slogan.

In order to dress appropriately, for all business occasions, it is important to understand the:

1. *Hierarchy of clothing:* The business suit for men and the skirt suit for women is still the most powerful look. I wear a skirt suit when meeting with a CEO for the first time. However, pantsuits have become very popular among women in business and there are some outstanding ones. In some

circumstances, they can convey the same power image as a skirt suit.

For men it's the sport jacket and trousers, followed by casual attire. For women, it's more complicated. After the skirt suit, if you are like me, it's the pantsuit or a dress with a jacket followed by mix-and-match slacks, skirts, blouses, and jackets, and dresses without jackets. Then it's casual clothing. These, of course, are general guidelines and unless you pay attention to the FACS (see below), you still won't know if what you are wearing is okay.

2. *FACS Method:* Regardless of what you are wearing, whether business or business casual dress, you want to pay attention to the FACS. FACS is an acronym that I developed to help people understand the basics about clothing and to help them develop their wardrobes.

   - *Fit*—Do your clothes fit properly? It doesn't matter how expensive something is. If it is too tight or too big, it isn't going to look good. Even more important, it's not going to look businesslike.

   - *Accessories*—Are your accessories too big, too bold, or too bright? Accessories should be good-quality items that add to your outfit without overpowering it. If you wear too many or if they are too strong, people may pay more attention to them than to you. This means no long nails with designs on them, jewelry that distracts, or scarves that overwhelm the outfit. Some years ago, there was a man in one of my classes I will never forget. He wore patterned suspenders, his ID was hanging on a plaid ribbon, his glasses hung from a chain, and he was wearing a brightly colored striped shirt. I confess I remember nothing he said or did that day—he had so much going on, it was hard even to look at him!

Pachter's Pointer: Watch it!

> The one accessory that almost everyone notices is your watch. Buy the most expensive one you can afford. You don't need a lot of different ones, you need one good-quality one. As the ad says, "It's your watch that tells the most about who you are."

- *Color*—Darker colors usually convey more authority than lighter ones, and bright colors may "shout." Make sure the colors you wear flatter you and say what *you* want them to say. (I am a tall person. I can't wear a two-piece red suit. If I did, you'd see me coming and going! That is not what I want to be remembered for. On the other hand, I can wear a red top and a dark bottom.)

- *Style*—Trendy clothes are certain to be noticed. For this reason, you won't be able to wear them as often. In addition, they could take attention away from you. As the saying goes, "Your clothes speak so loudly, I can't hear you." Usually classic, conservative clothing wears better, lasts longer, and doesn't go out of style as quickly.

Pachter's Pointer: If you break the rule, first know the rule, then break it well.

> Most TV interviewers wear suits. Larry King doesn't. By *not* wearing a jacket and making a point of wearing suspenders, he is sending a message and calling attention to himself. He does it so well that the suspenders have become his trademark. You, too, can break the rules, but *not* out of ignorance. You must *know* the image you are projecting and be certain that you can pull it off.

Oh, and *don't just tell me that you can pull it off*; get in-put from other people that tells you that you can pull it off.

When you break a rule and break it well, it becomes your trademark. When you break a rule and do it badly, you may not only be inappropriate, you may appear foolish. One woman who always wore very short skirts to work became known throughout the department as "Suzie short skirt"— *not* a good trademark! Even worse, people may think you are thumbing your nose at them.

3. *First impressions really do count,* and it's sometimes hard to change the message once implanted. First impressions are made within the first few seconds and a large part of what goes into a first impression is how you are dressed. My niece, a very professional young woman, dresses well. (Between her mom and me, she had no choice!) After one interview, the recruiter told her that the hiring manager said: "As soon as I saw her, I knew I would hire her."

Not too long ago, a young woman came to a colleague's office to apply for a position. It was raining. She wore a poncho with the hood pulled over her face. She looked like a little kid. A good raincoat and an umbrella would have looked more professional. Nevertheless, my colleague interviewed her, found she had a lot going for her, and hired her, but it was touch-and-go there for a while and, looking back, she said she may have given her a tougher interview than she would otherwise have.

4. *Build your wardrobe slowly.* When we're first starting out, we may not have much money to spend on clothing and accessories. You don't need a lot. Buy good, quality clothing and items that can be mixed and matched. Develop a relationship with a

salesperson at a good store. He or she will let you know when the clothing you like comes in or is on sale.

► **QUICK TIP:** Only buy something when it is on sale, if you would have bought it—had you been able to afford it—when it was full price.

All Business Casual Is Not Alike

Before their first meeting, Ryan was told by a client that theirs was a casual office and Ryan should come to meetings in business casual. Ryan believed that a suit and a tie was proper business attire and so wore a conservative suit to that first meeting. When scheduling their next meeting, which was to be attended by the division president, the client said, "Now remember, Ryan, we're a casual office—no suit and tie this time." Inexplicably, Ryan showed up in shorts, a T-shirt, and sneakers. When the client saw him, he immediately called the president and cancelled the meeting, and graciously gave Ryan one last warning.

What Went Wrong?

The client wanted Ryan to fit in, to be a part of his team. He had been told what to wear, and even if it wasn't his natural style, he needed to follow his client's lead. When he arrived dressed for a day in the park, he went to the other extreme. In both cases, he was not following the group's dress code and he paid a price for it. Actually, it could have been worse; he could've lost the account.

34. Rules of the business casual road.

1. *Know what your company allows.* Often these days, companies have written policies about what is and is not acceptable business casual attire. If your company does not have a written policy, look at what other people wear, especially the more

senior people, the more successful ones. They are often good role models.

 Pachter's Pointer: It's not fair but . . .

> And one more thing: It's not fair, I know, but in my opinion business casual can be more difficult for women. Men wear a pair of Dockers and a polo shirt, and it's fine.
>
> Women wear Dockers and a polo shirt and it's just not the same; it is way too casual because in many places it is still too easy to discount women. To make casual look professional, women usually need a second layer; for example, a jacket or sweater set. (I have been saying this ever since business casual exploded onto the workplace about ten years ago. It's interesting, back then some women didn't agree with me; today I don't hear any opposition!)

2. *Dress for the* particular *situation.* As Ryan learned the hard way, being too formally dressed was just as bad as being too informally dressed. Look at the people around you. Having once come too formally dressed, Ryan had the opportunity to see what the others were wearing. Apparently, he paid no attention, and therefore arrived underdressed for their second encounter. On the other hand, if you don't know what's right for a particular situation, ask someone who does.

▶ **QUICK TIP:** Although business casual is common in many offices throughout the United States, there still are many offices (or situations) where professional dress is essential and business suits are required for both men and women. Internationally, you may need more formal attire. Check before you go.

3. *Remember, neatness still counts.* Just because the occasion is casual, your clothing still needs to be cleaned and pressed. No holes, no frays.

- Casual for men includes casual slacks, Dockers, polo shirts, sweaters, long-sleeve shirts.

- Casual for women includes slacks, dresses and skirts (all lengths except mini), blouses, sweater sets, jackets.

▶ **QUICK TIP:** In some companies jeans are acceptable casual wear. If you do wear jeans, make sure they are clean and pressed.

 Pachter's Pointer: When in doubt, don't wear it.

If you have to ask yourself, should I or shouldn't I?—don't.

Sexy *Never* Says Corporate

A young manager for a large financial planning company wore a string bikini at her company picnic. No surprise—many of her male co-workers thought she looked fantastic. Her manager—the person who really counted—was appalled.

What Went Wrong?

Listen up, all you beautiful people who work out at the gym and like to show it off: Sexy is not an appropriate business look! Even if the event is *very* casual, it's still business and you must dress with business in mind. Two-piece suits, even if they're not string bikinis, may, like Janet Jackson's famous dress, malfunction, sometimes without any outside help. As one young woman told me, "I would never let my boss see me in a bikini; it would be like him seeing me half naked!"

And men, don't think you're immune. Speedos are inappropriate!

And, let's not forget: It's not only out-of-the-office attire that can be too sexy; what you wear *in* the office is equally important. I coached a young woman whose work was fine, but whose skirts were too short—four inches above her knees and so tight she couldn't bend over. No wonder she had been passed over for a promotion!

35. How not to send the wrong message.

1. *Don't flaunt your figure.* Or any part of your anatomy, for that matter. The office may be the last place standing where the saying "If you've got it, flaunt it" does not apply; at least not

when it comes to what you wear. Sexy is distracting; worse, it detracts from what you are saying and it affects how people perceive you. This is true for *both* men and women.

When dressing for the office, a business event, or a party ask yourself, "What am I drawing attention to?" and "What do I want to be remembered for?" If the answer to the first question is your fabulous legs or your muscled arms, return to your closet and begin again.

Pachter's Pointer: Sex appeal has its limits.

If your road to success is based on how sexy you look, you are dooming yourself to failure. Eventually, you won't be able to compete.

2. *Just say no to skintight outfits.* I am always amazed that I have to remind women that cleavage is not appropriate in the office. Other no-nos are high-slit skirts, short shorts or skirts, and wraparound skirts—they usually unwrap! You guys are not exempt: no muscle shirts and no shirts unbuttoned to the waist.

3. *No tattoos and no body piercings.* At least none that are visible in the office. This applies to both men and women. If your nose is pierced, please leave the ring at home.

4. *Jewelry is part of a woman's corporate uniform.* Earrings, a pin, a bracelet, or a necklace complete an outfit. But only in moderation. You don't want your jewelry to become a distraction. Don't wear anything that jangles or draws a lot of attention to itself. General guideline: one ring per hand (except a wedding set), one bracelet per arm. Jewelry for men, other than a watch and wedding or college ring, is not common in corporate America, though in some creative fields, you will, on occasion, see men with an earring or a bracelet.

5. *Keep your clothes on.* Really, this is not a joking matter. In my career, I've heard just about everything, but this story, which was told to me by an HR manager at a chemical company, beats all—and I mean *all*—of them. I wouldn't have believed it had I not known her for years.

As she told it, one of their saleswomen took a group of male clients out for cocktails and dinner at a wonderful Russian restaurant, complete with an authentic band and dancers. There was a lot of vodka and the music was infectious. Lydia was the only woman in the group and apparently enjoyed too much vodka because suddenly she ripped off her top and proceeded to dance on the tabletop. She was fired.

And that certainly is no joke!

Give Yourself the Great Grooming Edge

While waiting for a meeting to begin, Stan, a VP at a bank, opened his briefcase, took out a deodorant stick, unbuttoned his shirt, and proceeded to apply it, much to the astonishment of the woman next to him. Need I say it? She was shocked.

What Went Wrong?

While Stan's intentions were going in the right direction, his actions were not. And Stan's not the only one with the right impulse but the wrong action. One woman, who rushed to arrive at a banquet on time, pulled out a lint brush and proceeded to run it over a very elegant suit!

Grooming yourself in public is *not* okay. Although grooming is essential (it means paying attention to the little details that add polish to your professional presence), do it in the privacy of your own home, a restroom, or, if necessary, your office (but only with the door closed and preferably locked!).

This applies to putting on nail polish, lipstick, and other makeup. It also means you must not trim or file your nails. Although toothpicks are acceptable in some parts of the world, in the United States, they are not used in public. If food gets caught in your teeth, go to the restroom and remove it there. There is also no shaving in public. And speaking of shaving: no three-day stubble.

36. Corporate guide to good grooming.

1. *Use cologne or perfume sparingly.* This applies to both men and women. People have a tendency to use too much, which may put people off. There are also people who are allergic to cologne.

2. *Pay attention to your hair.* Your hair needs to be clean and styled to suit your face. As my mother would say, "You want to have a hair-*do*." This means both women *and* men, as a young man in a Prepare-to-Work program discovered. Before applying for an entry-level job at a prestigious hotel, his advisor told him to cut his hair—something the young man definitely did not want to do until the counselor explained, "It's not about your hair, it's about your career." He cut his hair, he got the job.

   - *Get a good haircut.* For both men and women, the style should be contemporary, but not extreme.

   - *No wild spikes or outlandish colors.* Red and blue hair may be patriotic, but it is not corporate.

   - *No long, flowing manes.* I know how possessive some people are about their hair, but please don't shoot the messenger! In today's corporate environment, long hair is just too sexy, too distracting, and, for women, too "little girl." Women with hair below the collar bone should pull it back, put it up, or cut it off. For you Samsons out there who won't cut off your locks, try a ponytail; but, I have to say, in my experience, few men can carry it off. If you can, and you are in an industry that will accept it, then you can give it a try.

Pachter's Pointer: For women only . . .

Make makeup part of your corporate uniform. It can pay real dividends. Women who wear makeup simply look more finished; more in control. You don't want to look like a painted doll, but a little lipstick, foundation and/or blush, and mascara go a long way.

If you don't know where to begin, go to a good cosmetics store or salon, and work with their makeup person. Just remember to tell her you want a look for business, not for an evening out.

I know one high-powered executive who got a huge promotion that she attributes to the moment she began wearing makeup to work. According to her, her work hadn't changed, but people just began to see her in a different light.

3. *Don't chew gum in public,* and don't let people know where you've hidden it!

4. *Skip the uninvited grooming assistance.* If ever there was a time to think before you act, this is it! The next time you're tempted to offer unsolicited help, remember to say *before you touch,* "The tag on your shirt is showing," "The zipper on the back of your dress is not zipped all the way," and then ask if you may help.

Don't Get Caught with Your Shoes Off!

In a recent training class, one young woman spent the session shoeless. At the end of the morning session, Lily got up to leave only to find that one shoe had gone missing. I guess the person next to her must have accidentally pushed it away when he got up during the break. It wasn't tragic, but she was embarrassed as everyone fell to their hands and knees to help her find it.

What Went Wrong?

It seems strange, even to me, that I have to say this, but you need to keep your shoes on. I have seen it too many times. I was sitting in the lobby of a Fortune 50 company waiting for someone when I noticed another woman sitting with her shoes off. The person she was to meet arrived before my contact did, so I was able to witness the look on the man's face as he watched her scramble into her shoes.

37. What your shoes say about you . . .

Some of us love shoes and can't have too many pairs—every style, every color; others don't care much about them as long as they are comfortable. Whichever side of the shoe equation you fall on, it's important to be aware of the impact shoes have on our professional image.

1. *People notice shoes.* They are one of those little details that say "professional." Therefore, they need to be in good condition, clean, and polished.

 Pachter's Pointer: For women only . . .

Heels are a part of the corporate uniform: generally, $1^1/_2$- to $2^1/_2$-inch heels, *not* spike heels. You guessed it—they are too sexy *and* they can hurt your feet! Similarly, no open-toe shoes or sandals, which tend not to convey a professional image. You don't want to hear, *"I love your toes!"* from some guy at a meeting or have him staring at your feet the whole time (a sales rep attending one of my seminars swore it happened to her).

2. *And speaking of shoes, what about socks?* Most often, it's men who ask if they have to wear socks. I usually respond, "I have to wear stockings, you have to wear socks." And although I know fewer and fewer women do, I encourage women to wear stockings.

Your Body Speaks a Thousand Words

A professor, a brilliant mathematician, swayed and played with the change in his pocket while teaching advanced calculus. It drove his students crazy!

What Went Wrong?

Posture can work for you or against you. It indicates how approachable you are, how confident you feel, and how nervous you are. The professor's body—his posture and gestures—not only conveyed nervousness, it distracted his students.

38. How to control what your body is saying.

1. *Reach for the sky.* You can stand tall no matter your height. Keep your head up and your chin level. Do not curve your back and pull your shoulders in. Stand with your back and shoulders straight. Your feet should usually be four to six inches apart.

▶ **QUICK TIP:** It's just as important to sit tall. Avoid slouching or slumping.

2. *Gesture effectively.* Gestures, used well, bring your words to life. When talking one on one, there are some common gestures you should try not to make:

- *Avoid nervous gestures.* No playing with pens or paper clips, tapping fingernails on tables, drilling with your feet, biting your lip, or wringing your hands. All of these make you seem uncomfortable or distracted.

- *Avoid pointing your finger or pounding the table.* These gestures make you seem aggressive, even if you only mean to be emphatic. Even though your words are fine, people will believe your gestures first. If you must point, keep your palm open and your fingers together.

- *Avoid arrogant gestures.* Snapping your fingers or lacing your hands behind your head distances you from people.

Pachter's Pointer: Comfortable or defensive?

Many of us fold our arms across our chests. Yet a viewer often takes it to mean the person is closed or defensive. Those who cross their arms often tell me they are more comfortable that way. While that may be true, consider which is more important: your comfort level or how people see you. I think the answer is obvious.

3. *Focus on the face.*

- *Look people in the eye. Don't* stare them down, and *do* occasionally look away. If you never look at people or look away most of the time, people will assume you are not listening, not believable, or simply nervous. (By the way, it's okay to be nervous; what's not okay is to let people know you are nervous. So look people in the eye; chances are they'll never guess you're feeling jittery.)

Pachter's Pointer: To see yourself as others see you . . .

Standard Facial Expression (SFE) is a phrase I coined to describe what people see when you are looking, listening, or just not saying anything. Some people's expressions are warm and friendly; others are stern and forbidding. It's obvious which face you want to cultivate.

One colleague actually stopped his presentation and asked a woman in the front row who had a very stern SFE, "Did I say something wrong; did I say something to offend you?" The woman was shocked; she had no idea she was sending such a negative message.

Occasionally, during a seminar, I look out at the first row, and based on the facial expressions I see, I think to myself, "These people hate me." I'm always wrong. These very same people are the ones who come up to me during the break and say, "Oh, gosh, Barbara, this is a great seminar!" I want to say to them, "Tell your face!" but I don't because I teach etiquette.

Listen Up!

Marcus, a young marketing supervisor, was being interviewed for a newly created position within his company. The manager was talking about the individuals in the department and mentioned one man that they both knew. He said, "He is really talented at—" Before he could finish his sentence, Marcus jumped in with, "—poker. We play every Friday night." The manager said coolly, "Oh. I was going to say data analysis. Do you always jump to conclusions?"

What Went Wrong?

Don't finish people's sentences for them. Marcus didn't allow his future boss to finish his thought before chiming in, and not only did he finish the sentence, he finished it incorrectly.

39. Six strategies for successful listening.

1. *Create a conducive environment.* Give the speaker your undivided attention. When possible, close any doors, turn off any music, and don't answer your phone. It destroys any rapport you are trying to create.

2. *Be aware of your body language.* As mentioned earlier, body language is important. Look at the person. Make sure your facial expression is appropriate for the discussion. Don't cross your arms, which may appear defensive. Let the other person you are talking to see that you are paying attention.

3. *Stop talking!* This may be the hardest to do! Let the other person talk, and don't interrupt. (See Part 5 for more information on interrupting.)

4. *Don't leap to a conclusion or cut the conversation short.* Let the person explain his or her thought fully before you respond. Ask questions if there's something you don't understand. And keep an open mind.

5. *Make sure that what you* thought *you heard is what was meant.* You do this by "checking in." Don't do it too often, but if done occasionally checking in really shows that you are listening. Try using phrases like these:

   If I understand you correctly, you are suggesting . . .
   You are saying . . .
   Let me make sure I'm clear. You . . .

6. *Verbal prompts.* Verbal prompts are another way to let the speaker know you are paying attention. They are particularly important on the phone, where the speaker cannot read your body language. Verbal prompts are not filler words. Some verbal prompts are:

   "Okay . . ."
   "I see."
   "Yes."
   "That's true."

SPEAK THE PART: COMMUNICATE YOUR IMAGE—WITH WORDS

If You Speak, But Aren't Heard . . .

John, a laboratory assistant, kept telling his supervisor, Melanie, "I can't hear you," whenever she gave him instructions. The lab, filled with fans and manufacturing equipment, was very noisy, but she never raised her voice. It was very frustrating for both of them: for him, because he couldn't hear her, and for her, because she had to repeat everything she told him several times. The subject came up during his six-month review, and he finally said (only half jokingly), "I guess either you're going to learn how to speak up or we're both going to have to learn sign language."

What Went Wrong?

Melanie is not aware of how softly she is speaking and how ineffective it makes her seem. Volume is one of those little things that make a big difference in how you are perceived. If you speak softly or you don't project your voice, it is easy for others not to pay attention to you. In my book, projecting your voice is among the top things a person needs to do to appear professional.

40. How to make sure your words get through.

1. *Speak up.* Do people often say, "I can't hear you," or have you ever said to yourself, "I thought I just said that," as someone

repeats a point you'd made? Chances are you were not speaking with enough volume so other people *really* heard you. If this happens to you, it's time to raise your volume.

The recording secretary of a large organization can't hear one of the regular participants in their weekly meetings. She asks him to speak up. He doesn't. She asks again; he doesn't. Eventually, she stops recording his comments.

If he has anything worthwhile to contribute, no one will ever know. Everyone loses. Many people who speak softly don't realize how low their volume is. Some, like this man, are virtually inaudible. Sometimes they believe that if they raise their voices, they'll be shouting. That is rarely the case.

If you are asked to repeat yourself or speak up, chances are that you are just not used to speaking louder. If that's the case, try this simple 1-2-3-4-5 exercise. Say 1 at your softest volume and as you count to 5, raise your voice so that when you reach 5, you are the loudest you can be. Most people's volume should fall between the 2½ and 3½ level.

2. *Pay attention to your diction.* We make assumptions about people based on how *clearly* they *pronounce* and how *correctly* they *use* words. If your diction is poor, people often make negative assumptions.

   Two common errors will give you an idea of what I mean:

   - *Youse.* There is no plural for *you* other than *you!* A new colleague went up to two teammates at a meeting and said, "What are youse guys doing about the proposal?" What? Where did he go to school? They immediately questioned his ability.

     A partner in an accounting firm transferred a recently hired accountant from a fast-track position to an inside job, because the new man continued to say "youse" even after being told about it. The partner was embarrassed to have him represent the firm to clients.

- *Gonna and gotta.* Listen to the difference. Which sounds more professional?
  "We are gonna do this and you gotta attend the meeting."
  or
  "We are going to do this and you have to attend the meeting."

3. Don't *upspeak.* This is a relatively new phenomenon. Some say it began with the Valley Girls. I hear it more and more. At first, mostly young women were doing it, now I hear people of all ages and both sexes upspeaking. It's the way some people have of making a declarative sentence, "I think we should begin the marketing campaign for the new multimillion-dollar gizmo on Tuesday," end with a question mark. Their voices rise instead of fall at the end of the sentence. It makes the speaker sound tentative, uncertain of him- or herself, and if you do it, it detracts from your credibility.

▶ **QUICK TIP:** Remember to say "please" and "thank you." It always amazes me that I have to remind people to say these words, but I do; in, turn, you'll be amazed at how much better people hear you when you start using these three little words. This lesson was brought home to me recently when Jesse, an administrative assistant who works for four bosses, told me that when she has work to be done for more than one, the boss who says "please" gets his or her work done first.

"I Don't Know How to Say This": Finding the Right Words

During a meeting with 10,000 employees, James, COO of a large company, used a number of highly descriptive curse words in his presentation. He may have thought it made him sound like "just folks," but the key thing his audience came away with—and all they talked about—was his language. He blew it.

What Went Wrong?

Whatever your place in the corporate pecking order: no cursing, no exceptions. You lose the respect of others, and, unless you own the company, it can be costly to your career. In fact, even if you do own the company, it can cost you customers and set a very bad example for your employees.

41. Words and phrases to avoid.

1. *Hedges.* These are extra words like *kinda, sorta, maybe, perhaps, actually* that we add to our sentences. Like upspeak, they diminish what we are saying by making us sound uncertain. They are not necessary. They *kinda* take away from what you are saying.

   And then there is *I think.* When you say "I think," you are telling people you don't *know*. Some people do this, even when they know (afraid being sure makes them seem arrogant). As a result, they lose power. If, for example, you are asked which vendor to use, and you have an opinion, say, "I recommend" or "I suggest" rather than "I think."

Same is true of "We are trying to . . ." Imagine this scenario:

Betsy, a VP of a marketing firm, is at a meeting with clients, who were over budget and behind schedule. Her purpose: to reassure the client that all would be well. She begins her presentation: "We are trying to . . ." and ends with, "I think we will meet the deadline." I am sure you'll believe the punch line: Her firm lost the client and Betsy lost her job.

2. *Fillers.* These are simply extra words that clutter our sentences. We don't pause, but instead add words and sounds: *Um, you know, all right, okay.* You don't need to be perfect; an occasional *um* or *okay* is rarely noticed, but when it becomes a pattern, people do notice and, if it's very frequent, they may stop listening and start counting!

Pachter's Pointer: Listen to your voicemail message.

Do you use filler words? What are they? Rerecord the message. Listen as you speak with friends and colleagues, at meetings, in front of groups. Once you become aware of the fillers you use, over time you can eliminate them. (This exercise will also help you learn about other word choices you make.)

3. *Spilling.* Don't point out tiny flaws in yourself that if you didn't draw attention to, no one would notice. It can destroy people's confidence in you. Become aware of using such phrases as "I am not any good at . . ." and "I am really terrible with . . ."

4. *Details (in moderation only, please).* People tune out if you go too heavy on the details. We have all met someone like this—if

you ask this guy the time, he will build you the watch. Say what you need to say in as few as words as possible. This means, don't use:

- too many facts

- too many words

    For example, instead of saying:
    "The paper I just read talks about or explains the new additions to the budget; by which I mean, the line items we didn't have in last year's budget."
    say
    "The paper discusses the new budget items."

5. *"But" out.* When people hear "but," it makes everything said before it appear negative. When someone says "I agree but," she doesn't really agree; if he says "You did a good job, but"— you are waiting for the bad news. That's what happened to Felicia. She sat down expecting a good review, and immediately her boss said, "I'd love you to be a member of my team forever, *but* I need to ask you a question." Suddenly, certain she was going to be fired, tears welled up in Felicia's eyes. She loved this job. Actually, her boss was going to say, "How would you feel about moving to Chicago? They've got an opening for a plant manager. It would be a promotion and an awfully nice salary increase." Every time she saw him, she never left him forget it. Replace "but" with "and," and you'll see positive results.

6. *"I'm sorry."* Wait a minute. Let me explain. I am not telling you to be rude. I am not talking about genuine "I'm sorrys." For example, if you spill coffee in your boss's lap or you trip a

coworker as you rush past with the latest sales figures, express your sympathy and be sorry! Instead, I am talking about the use of "I'm sorry" that:

- *Puts you down.* For example, using sentences like: "I am sorry to bother you," or "I'm sorry, I need to talk to you." Why be sorry? Instead of "I'm sorry" try "Excuse me, I would like to talk to you about . . ."

- *Takes responsibility for something that is not your fault.* When you do this, the listener—boss, client, colleague— then associates you with the negative thing that happened. For example, a manager said to a client when she was delayed to a meeting, "I'm sorry the traffic was so bad." Why is the manager sorry?

  If you say, "I'm sorry the project is behind schedule," you are implying it's your fault that the project is behind schedule. You can acknowledge the difficulty by saying something such as: "The project is behind schedule and we are working as fast as we can to get it back on schedule." If you have had people say to you, "Why are you sorry?" or "Don't be sorry," chances are you are taking responsibility for something that wasn't your fault.

Other phrases to avoid

- *"I'll be honest with you . . ."* Does it mean you weren't honest before?

- *"I don't know."* I *am not* talking about saying "I don't know" when you don't know the answer, as in, "What time is the meeting?" I *am* talking about adding "I don't know" when you *do* know. For example, "I would like to use XYZ supplier. They have great prices. Oh, I don't know. What do you think?" It makes you appear unsure of yourself or unsure of what are you saying when you really do know.

"It's Not Funny!":
Inappropriate Humor

One Halloween, a pharmaceutical sales representative dressed as the Grim Reaper went into the intensive care unit of a hospital! He was trying to be funny. Neither the patients nor the hospital staff was amused. Neither was the representative's boss when she learned the representative was ordered to leave the building.

What Went Wrong?

Humor can add a lot to your life, conversations, and presentations. It can break the ice, warm up an audience, and generally take the edge off tense moments. But if you don't do it right, humor can bomb badly. When it does, not only won't you get a laugh, it can *really* backfire and embarrass or offend others. Follow the guidelines below and you won't look like a jerk when you're trying to be funny.

42. The four "serious" rules of humor.

1. *Think before you act!* It sounds simple, doesn't it? "Think before you act" may be the hardest lesson to learn about humor. All too often, something comes into our heads; we think it's clever or cute, and without giving it a second thought, it becomes mother to the deed. And then it's too late.

   Before you do something that is different or out of the ordinary—no matter how funny you think it is, ask yourself these three questions:

• How would others view what I am doing?

• How would I feel if someone did this to me?

• Could I tell my mother what I had done?

If the representative had done this, chances are he would have realized that his prank would flop and reflect badly on both him and his company.

2. *Avoid sex, politics, and religion.* We said it before and we'll say it again. Avoid these topics. Period. End of discussion. This rule not only applies to business situations, it applies to most social situations as well.

This was never clearer to me than when I heard about a marketing VP who began his welcoming speech at a weekend retreat for the launch of a new product with a sexist joke. Jaws literally dropped in shock and outrage. Later, the jawing was nonstop: "How could he tell *that* joke? Is he out of his mind?" Which subject got the most attention—the new product launch or the story—is not hard to guess. The retreat was intended to be motivational and an opportunity for team building. One bad joke had precisely the opposite effect.

3. *Don't make fun of others.* You don't know whose mother worked where and whose grandfather did what. What's more, it is just *not* nice.

As I travel around the country, I have noticed that people in one part of the country more and more often will make fun of others from a different area. It's not funny, and can be downright dangerous to your career. After all, you never know where that important client was born until you say the wrong thing about his hometown.

4. *Don't force humor.* If you are uncomfortable telling a story or not good at it—and not all of us are—don't do it! If ever in doubt, don't. I know it does seem unfair that some people have a natural gift for humor. Admire them, laugh with them, and learn from them.

PART FOUR

Techno- and Retro-Etiquette: Getting Your Message Across in a 24/7 World

The way we communicate in the workplace has changed dramatically over the last twenty years. There are new communication technologies, like email and cell phones, that allow us to communicate more conveniently and rapidly than ever before. Eight out of ten cell phone users say that the phones have made their lives easier and six in ten say that email has made their lives easier, according to a 2005 University of Michigan poll.

Despite the widespread use of these devices, some people still haven't learned to use the technologies well and therefore may come across as rude, although that's usually the

last thing in the world they intend. It's not because they are deliberately being rude, they just don't realize that, like the older forms of
communication—the typed letter, the handwritten note, the telephone, and face-to-face conversation—etiquette is essential to the
new technologies. What is appropriate for each may vary somewhat
(and we'll be looking at the differences and similarities), but because of their speed, etiquette may be even more essential than
before.

As with all things new, there is a learning curve. New technology
appears and it takes us time to understand the good and not so good
about it. Slowly, guidelines are established—people learn from their
mistakes, etiquette experts also weigh in—and over time we learn
how to use the technology politely. Even the CEO of IBM wouldn't
have known what was needed thirty years ago; these technologies
simply didn't exist!

This new field of techno-etiquette includes email, voicemail, cell
phones and the myriad other devices available today (and those that
will become available tomorrow). Yet regardless of the technology,
there are two key things to consider:

1. What image are you projecting?

2. How will the way you use the technology affect others?

As you can judge from these questions, the goals of communication are the same regardless of the technology used to transmit the
message, and, because retro forms of communication are still an important part of the way we communicate, we'll include some reminders throughout this section on how to use them well.

Before you begin, let's find out how techno savvy you are.

Techno Savvy Self-Assessment Challenge: How techno savvy are you?

Assign a number to each item using this scale of 1 to 5 (1 = Never, 5 = Often).

_____ 1. Have you been asked to lower your voice when using a cell phone?

_____ 2. Have you accidentally sent an email to someone other than the intended recipient?

_____ 3. When talking on your cell phone has someone in the vicinity responded to your conversation as if you were talking to him or her?

_____ 4. Does your voicemail message contain outdated information?

_____ 5. Do you answer your cell phone when engaged in a face-to-face conversation with another person?

_____ 6. Do you leave voicemail messages that say, "Hi. It's me. Call me."?

_____ 7. Have you accidentally sent an email before you were finished writing and proofreading the message?

_____ 8. Have you left a voicemail message for someone without leaving your phone number?

_____ 9. Do you keep your cell phone headset on when you are not using the phone?

_____ 10. Have you answered your telephone in front of other people?

_____ 11. Is your voicemail box/email box usually full, making it impossible for callers/emailers to leave a message?

_____ 12. Do you usually skip reading the manuals and avoid staying up-to-date with the latest technology?

Total Score:_____ (See below to find out how techno savvy you are.)

Your Techno Savvy Scorecard

• If your total is 12 to 24, you are a Techno Maven! You usually handle technology well and appear polite when communicating with others.

• If your total is 24 to 36, you often handle technology well and appear polite when communicating with others.

Okay, you've done well, but hold on. Before you skip ahead to the next chapter thinking you know all you need to know, remember that this is *your* perception of you. Other people may see you differently! I encourage you to read on and find out.

• If your total is 36 to 48, you can handle technology well, but can have difficulty using technology to communicate with others; you may appear impolite at times.

• If your total is 48 or higher, you frequently have difficulty using technology to communicate with others and seem impolite at times.

Before You Press "Send": Email Embarrassments and Other Faux Pas

Carina, the manager of a hospital lab, emailed a coworker to vent about her workload and the extra hours she was putting in. She had let Joan, her administrative assistant, go because, she said, Joan was lazy. She *still* believed that Joan was lazy, but, Carina said, she had underestimated how much "the little" that Joan did actually helped her. Accidentally, Carina sent the email to everyone in her address list—which included Joan's home email address! Perhaps you can imagine Carina's embarrassment when Joan emailed a reply to the entire list that included a laundry list of Carina's faults!

What Went Wrong?

Of course, it is inappropriate to say negative things to coworkers about colleagues—past or present—whatever technology you are using. However, the risks multiply when you use email. If you make a mistake, as Carina did, you can really end up embarrassing yourself and others.

Email is so easy to use that we often don't think about what we are doing (or saying), and, of course, with a mere "slip of the finger," it's so simple to hit the wrong key, and *whoosh!* off it goes. When using email, pay attention; do nothing by rote.

At the same time, you may push the wrong button because you don't know how to properly use your equipment. It's very important

BLUNDER BUSTER

If Carina had realized her mistake, she could have tried the recall button—if her system had one. Even if it did, the recall function may not recall the message in time. What's more, not all systems will accept a "recall," especially from a different internet service provider (ISP).

An HR administrator I know accidentally sent an email that listed everyone's salary. She tried to recall the message, but it was too late. She followed up with an email asking people not to read the original email. *Right!*

You can learn from her mistake. In the future make sure you 1) use the technology correctly; 2) think carefully about what you've said before pressing the Send button; and 3) avoid gossip or talking badly about someone, particularly in an email.

to learn how to use the technology well. Read the manual. Take a training class if one is offered. Make certain you know which buttons to push! Not knowing can create problems and embarrassment— for yourself and others.

43. Email manners matter.

1. *No X-rated, offensive, or sexist communications.* To put it bluntly: They are not nice—whether they are sent techno or retro!

A seminar attendee told me this story: A young man sent an email to a friend at his former job boasting about his new job, the money he was now earning, and—for good measure—the women at the new company. He claimed they were so much better—sexier, prettier, flirtier—than those at the old one. His friend thought the email was obnoxious and forwarded it to everyone at the old company, including the women! You can bet he'll never get another reference from anyone at that firm, and, as we all know, word spreads quickly throughout an industry.

If that doesn't do it for you, remember emails can be easily forwarded to people you wouldn't want to read the message. Still not convinced? How's this: People have been fired as a result.

A word to the wise: Keep this advice in mind when you use the Internet at work. Do not pull up inappropriate websites. Some employers have strict rules and controls about using the Internet for personal business of any nature, and some monitor the sites their employees visit.

2. *Don't say anything you wouldn't say to the person's face.* Email should *never* be used to transmit bad news or to fire someone. Used appropriately, email can be incredibly efficient, and an email can sometimes get through when other methods of communication are down. During the 2005 bombing of the London subway, when regular phone lines and cell phones were overloaded, a newscaster encouraged people to use email to get in touch with their loved ones.

3. *If you don't want it known, don't send it.* Email isn't always private. Your company can and will monitor your use of email. Ask yourself, "Do I want my boss to read this email?" It's also good to be aware that the Delete button doesn't really delete the message. A techie can ferret out the message, if it comes to that.

4. *Remember, email can leave a trail.* This last point was dramatically brought home to me not long ago. A colleague had

emailed to inquire about the status of her invoice. The accounts payable person, Sarah, forwarded the email to the head of her department asking, "What should I say? It's nearly sixty days old." The department head emailed back, "Stall them, we're short of cash this month; we'll pay next month." Sadly, when Sarah replied, she automatically forwarded the whole series of emails! Of course, my colleague never said anything and they did pay the following month. So, in this case, all's well that ends well, but it could have been a much more serious series of emails that fell into unintended hands.

▶ **QUICK TIP:** Instead of pressing Reply to the email, start a new one.

5. *Take a breath.* Don't send an email (or leave a voice message) in anger. It is too easy to regret afterward. Put it aside—if you can—for at least twenty-four hours; if it can't wait a day, wait at least an hour.

6. *Don't use email to solve complex issues.* We've all had the experience: One email leads to another and the trail goes on and on. When the issues get complicated or the topic is touchy, set up a face-to-face meeting. If the person isn't nearby, the telephone may be a good substitute.

   This can be even more important when more than two people are involved:

   Two teams were having a hard time finding common ground on a number of issues that affected the high-priority project they were working on. Most of their discussions were via email. Weeks went by and everyone was getting testy when the project manager finally called a meeting. The problems were resolved in a matter of minutes and good working relationships were reestablished.

▶ **QUICK TIP:** None of the new communication technologies replaces face-to-face communication. One company established a policy of no internal emails on Fridays to encourage team-building and reduce conflict. It worked.

 Pachter's Pointer: Answer in kind.

If someone emails, reply by email; if a person phones, return the call. You can assume that the person prefers the form of communication he or she uses; responding in the same way follows the person's preference.

Some Things Change, Some Don't: The Anatomy of an Email

At one of my seminars not too long ago, I asked what people liked and didn't like about email. Hilda, a seemingly mild-mannered manager of a mid-sized company, waved frantically to be recognized. Obviously, something about email touched a nerve. When I called on her, it was as if a dam had broken. She couldn't get the words out fast enough. She was simply sick and tired of the rudeness of most people—sending emails without so much as a "Dear Hilda." "Where were they brought up?" she wondered self-righteously.

What Went Wrong?

Some people are annoyed when an email does not include a greeting. How could people be so rude? In fact, they and Hilda are incorrect. People aren't being rude; they simply are following the "retro" guidelines for writing a memo, which requires no salutation or closing, just the "to," "from," and "subject" lines.

Over time email users started adding greetings to their emails, probably because they felt their messages seemed too impersonal without one. By adding a salutation, what once was a memo has become a "mini-letter," meaning you are placing a letter inside the memo, and it's a little more formal as a result.

44. Guidelines (not hard-and-fast rules) for emailers.

1. *To, CC, and BCC*

- *Don't add to the flood of email.* Send your messages only to those who *really* need the information. Hard to believe, I know, but studies show that instead of saving time, email causes people to work one to two extra hours a day.

- *Only CC people with a need to know.* Your boss or your boss's boss doesn't need to see every message you send. Neither do colleagues. Think twice before deciding to whom you are sending what messages.

- *Don't use CCs as a subtle way to send negative messages* (or to win brownie points). An attendee at one of my seminars told me that her boss sends reminders to staff members when they are late on a project and copies those who are on time. As she put it, "No one likes being reprimanded in public." It's also bad manners.

 Pachter's Pointer: CC when you have something nice to say.

A great way to say thank you to your team (and give yourself a subtle pat on the back) is to send an email to your entire team congratulating them on a job well done—under budget and ahead of schedule—and copying the boss. Your staff will appreciate that the boss knows they did a good job, and you'll have tooted your own horn without looking like you were taking all the credit.

- *Use BCC to protect recipients' privacy.* Blind CCs are used primarily to keep a recipient's name secret from the others

to whom the email is sent. Since you are hiding information, its use in business is limited to special circumstances;
for example, if you want to keep an independent confidential record of your email.

 Pachter's Pointer: Add the email address last.

Add it only when you are ready to send the email. That way
you won't inadvertently send an email before you have finished writing and proofreading it. Even when you are replying to a message, it's a good precaution to delete the
address and insert it after you've reread and proofed it. It
really is worth the extra few seconds it takes.

2. *The subject line.*

- *Always use a targeted subject line.* Some people won't even
  open an email that doesn't have a subject line; others decide
  whether or not to open an email based on its subject line.
  It's not that they are being rude, but with so many emails
  each day, many people only open messages that seem to apply to them and skip those that don't.

- *Use a subject line to convey the whole message.* This can
  be effective if the message is short. One man adds ^eom^ to
  let people know that the subject is the end of message, so
  they don't spend time opening the email looking for the rest
  of the message.

3. *The salutation.*

- *Internal email:* No salutation needed, but you might want
  to add something simple like (in order of increasing formality): "Hi," "Sally," or "Hi, Sally," or "Dear Sally."

- *External email:* Use a greeting. "Hi, Tom," or "Dear Tom" or, more formally, "Dear Mr. Jones."

4. *The message (or body).*

- *Keep it to one subject.*

- *Pay attention to how it looks.* Make it easy to read. The general guideline is no more than twenty-five lines, or one computer screen. Use short paragraphs and blank lines between paragraphs. Use bullets. This is especially important if the email is long.

- *Use your favorite word processing system.* Some email systems let you use your preferred word processing system to write emails; on other systems, you can use your preferred word processing program and copy it into an email message. Most word processing systems have better grammar and spelling checkers, which makes it easier to check your message for errors.

▶ **QUICK TIP:** Put the most important information up front.

5. *The closing.*
    If you used a salutation, you need a closing. Usually "Regards," "Best regards," or if using last names, "Sincerely" is fine.

6. *The signature.*
    Include your full name, title, company name, web address, email, and phone number. If you get a lot of faxes, include a fax number. Also a one-line marketing plug may be included, but keep it to one line, not a whole paragraph!

"But It's Casual" Doesn't Cut It: Quality Counts

To: Staff
From: Phil
It has come to my attention lately that some of the devises have been defective. QUALTY counts. I want to remind the entire staff that zero defect are our goal.
T hankx. Phil

His staff thought it was a joke. Not only was Phil sure he had lost credibility with them, but word of what he'd done had percolated through the ranks—up and down. He still hasn't heard the end of it!

What Went Wrong?

Email is a written document and even though it is an informal, quick means of communication, it still says something about you. Therefore, the quality of your writing *always* matters. In this case, Phil was trying to make a very important point about the importance of quality, but the quality of his writing sent a very different message, and he lost credibility as a result. You don't want to inadvertently make an error and undermine your image and ideas.

45. Writer's rules of the road.

1. *Keep your writing simple, clear, and direct.* Write in a conversational style. Your goal is to be understood.

BLUNDER BUSTER

Admit your mistake.

Call a meeting of your entire staff and apologize for the email. Use the opportunity to stress the importance of quality assurance. And, in the future, pay attention to these writing guidelines.

2. *Looks count.* Break up your paragraphs. Long sentences or paragraphs are more difficult to read. Vary the length of your sentences and paragraphs. They add visual interest to your document and make it more appealing.

3. *Use simple and clear words.* Why say "annihilate" when "eliminate" or "get rid of" will do?

4. *Eliminate extra words.* "The most valuable of all talents is that of never using two words when one will do," said Thomas Jefferson. And the author of the Declaration of Independence should surely know. One of the biggest complaints people have about other people's writing is that they use too many words! Shorter documents are more likely to be read. Use as many words as necessary and no more.

5. *Don't use the CAPS LOCK.* Using all capital letters is the written equivalent of shouting. What's more, it's difficult to read. (Don't use all lowercase either; that, too, is hard to read.)

6. *Use abbreviations carefully* and only when you are certain your recipient will understand them. My assistant recently received an email that kept referring to 1Q. It took her a few

seconds to figure it out. It stood for first quarter, a common abbreviation in accounting and financial circles, but not so common in the world of corporate training.

Be especially careful about abbreviations when your recipients are not from the United States. The abbreviation may not make sense to those from other countries.

7. *Proofread everything.* Your email should have no mistakes when you send it (for more on proofreading, see the next section).

"Just the Fonts, Ma'am":
Check and Double-Check

Wesley, who was looking for freelance work, sent an email to Theresa, a marketing consultant. He had cut and pasted pieces from previous emails, but, sadly, the fonts and type sizes varied from email to email. Theresa deleted the message without even replying.

What Went Wrong?

It is very easy to cut and paste bits and pieces from one email to the next, but this doesn't mean you don't have to look at the result. The originals may have been fine on their own; but together, as in Wesley's email, the result was a mess. Wesley did not proofread his message, and, as a result, Theresa thought Wesley was sloppy and not even worth replying to.

Emails, like any other communication, must be proofread. Spelling and grammar count. A thoughtful, well-written email, like a carefully written letter, shows that you respect the recipient and that you have taken the time and made the effort to show that you care about your work.

46. Don't let your computer wreck your image.

1. *Print it out.* Whether you are writing an email or any other document, proofread the hard copy. It is much harder to see your mistakes on screen. If you get and send as much email as

I do, you may not be able to do this for every email you write; it is too time-consuming. But for important messages, it is worth this extra step.

2. *Read it aloud.* And read slowly; you are more apt to catch your mistakes. You can also have someone else look at it for you. A fresh set of eyes can often see mistakes you missed.

 Pachter's Pointer: Always look for one.

> When you proof, say to yourself there has to be at least one error. Look for it and you will usually find it.

3. *Learn from your frequent errors.* What mistakes do you make most often? We all do it. There are certain words we habitually misspell, typos we repeatedly trip over, and words we misuse. If you make a written or mental note of your mistakes, after a while, you will automatically look for them and make sure you've gotten them right!

4. *Check any numbers.* It can cost you a lot if you don't. Most of us don't type numbers often and, as a result, type them incorrectly.

5. *Use spell-check every time.* Word processing programs and some email programs allow you to do this automatically. Automatic or not, do it; it's worth the extra time and effort.

And cut the cutesy spellings from emails. A business email is not the place to be cute. An executive I know uses "Thanx" at the end of her messages. *Wrong!* It's too informal. That goes double for smileys and emoticons. They are way too informal for business.

6. *Keep a good style sheet or grammar guide and dictionary* at your fingertips and use it (you can even access some good ones

on the Internet). If you are unsure whether something is correct, look it up.

Pachter's Pointer: Your computer is not *always* right.

No computer grammar- or spell-checker is correct 100 percent of the time. A word can be spelled correctly; for example, *their* and *there* or *your* and *you're*, but used incorrectly. Most checkers won't catch this type of error, so be sure to proofread your messages carefully before you press that Send key!

The same is true of grammar; checkers are good, but they don't catch everything, especially if your sentence is complicated. Sometimes they suggest changes that make no sense in the context of what you are saying. Worst of all, in some cases, the changes they suggest are downright wrong.

Pachter's Pointer: Email Style FAQS.

These questions have come via email:

1. *What color ink and font size is acceptable in business? I haven't been able to find this information anywhere. Help.*

2. *My boss uses red and boldface for all his emails. I don't like it; I feel like I'm being yelled at. Is this correct?*

With all the options available on our computers, what should you do? There's boldface and italics; you can also underscore; you can use different-size fonts and colors. I once received this email:

*THANK YOU so much for your quick response. I would love to get **all** the <u>complete brochure outlines</u> on your **Corporate Training** seminars for both the $1/2$ day and full day sessions.*

What you can't see is that the writer used purple. A bit much for a simple request, don't you think?

It is important that what you write is easy to read. Using large fonts, very small fonts, and different colors makes it difficult for people to quickly read the message. Black ink is appropriate for all business writing—including email. Generally it is best to use 10- or 12-point type and an easy-to-read font, such as Arial or Times New Roman.

Also, use only one font. Whatever font you choose, be consistent throughout the message. Last, but not least, boldface or italics should be used sparingly.

Brrrring!!!!: To Answer or Not to Answer

Keith, a manager at a telecommunications company, was in his office meeting with a counterpart from another division. They were discussing how their departments might work together on an upcoming project. When Keith's phone rang, he answered the call and proceeded to have a ten-minute conversation. As he sat there, Morrie, the manager of the other department, could tell it was not an emergency call and was furious at the way he was treated. No surprise that it took them longer to reach some common ground on how to work together.

What Went Wrong?

The telephone is not new technology. It's been around for a long time, but there is still one major blunder people make—and that is answering the phone, land line or cell, in the presence of others.

I am simply amazed at the number of top-notch professionals I've coached who do not know that it's very rude to answer the phone and conduct a conversation when another person is in his or her office. Think about it: What's your visitor to do? Sit there and try to disappear into the wall? Pretend not to be eavesdropping? Walk out? When you answer the phone and have a conversation, you are "telling" the visitor that the caller is more important than he or she is.

When someone is in your office, let the message go to your voicemail. The same is true if you receive a call on your cell; if you are having lunch or meeting out of your office, turn the ringer off and let

BLUNDER BUSTER

Take action.

If you're expecting an important call, for example, an overseas call from your boss, then you need to "pre-call" it—let your visitor know when he or she enters your office that you are expecting an important call and that you will need to interrupt the meeting if it comes through.

If you forget to do this at the start of the meeting, when the phone rings, say something like, "Oh, I forgot to tell you that I was expecting a call from Melanie (if your guest doesn't know who Melanie is, also identify her as the president of the company, and explain that she is overseas), and I must take this call."

▶ **QUICK TIP:** The same is true of a cell call, except it's best to turn off the ring and put it on vibrate if you are with another person.

it go to voicemail. Pick up messages promptly after your meeting has ended.

47. Techno or retro, when answering the phone . . .

1. *Let it ring at least once before answering it.* If you pick the phone up mid-ring, you may make your caller uncomfortable. People expect the phone to ring.

2. *Answer with a greeting;* for example, your name and/or company name or department. Give both your first and last name.

    "Good morning. Pachter & Associates. Joyce Hoff speaking."

    "Good afternoon. Barbara Pachter speaking."

3. *Pay attention to your voice.* Speak clearly and not too quickly. Do not eat or drink when speaking on the phone.

48. When placing a call . . .

1. *Identify yourself immediately.*

2. *Err on the side of formality.* If you are unsure whether to use a person's first or last name, use the last name. Do not shorten a person's name or use a nickname. You can always work your way down; it's a lot harder to work your way back up. Outside the United States, where business relationships are generally more formal, this is particularly important.

3. *If you dial a wrong number, apologize.* Not only is it the right thing to do, but, with caller ID or *69, it's easy for the person on the other end to find you and/or your number.

 Pachter's Pointer: Return telephone calls within twenty-four hours.

In some industries, however, calls must be returned immediately, or it can cost you business.

And while we are on the subject of wrong numbers . . .

Ralph called 800-555-1212 to get a client's toll-free number. The client's headquarters were located in New Mexico. The operator told Ralph to call the number for international directory assistance. Thinking the operator had not heard him, Ralph repeated his request for New Mexico. Still, he was told to call international. Finally, Ralph asked to speak to the operator's supervisor.

The operator apparently did not know his own country's geography. Knowing your own country's geography and time zones is particularly important when doing business internationally. Whether it's making calls and understanding time differences, or the need to dial country codes before the rest of the number, or knowing a country's Internet code, it's important to acquaint yourself with the little details.

Just imagine how frustrated a visitor to the United States from another country might get had he called for a number in New Mexico and been told to call international. If he didn't know better, he would, and once he'd reached the international operator, he'd be told to call the United States operator.

"But It's Playing My Song": Manners Matter More Than Ever (or At Least As Much) on Your Cell

Neal was giving a quality orientation presentation to a large group in an auditorium. His cell phone, which was in his pocket, rang in the middle of the presentation. As he took the call, he told his audience, "Sorry, I have to take this," spoke for just a few seconds, and then continued his presentation. Needless to say, he lost his audience in just those few seconds. What made things even worse, his presentation was being videotaped for an international audience!

What Went Wrong?

People have become addicted to their phones. The rules that apply to retro phone use apply equally to techno phones. Just as you should not answer your phone except in an emergency when someone is in your office, you should not answer your cell phone when you are with another person or group of people. When you answer your phone at inappropriate times, you look foolish. Worse, it can cost you business.

 Pachter's Pointer: If it's still an issue in your organization . . .

When you are in a meeting, politely remind attendees to turn off their phones. One prominent real estate organization charges people $5 every time their cell phone rings during their monthly meeting. The money goes to charity.

49. Suggestions I never thought I'd have to make.

1. *Do not use your phone in the bathroom!* Ugh! Why do I have to say this? Because it happens; trust me, it really does happen. No one wants to be on the other end of a flushing toilet.

2. *Put your phone on vibrate.* A man came up to me at the beginning of a class and said that since this was an etiquette class he wanted to tell me that he was leaving his phone on because he was expecting an important call from his daughter. He said he would take the call and leave the room. I thanked him, adding, "I assume the phone will be on vibrate." "Oh no," he said, "I don't know how to do that!"

   I said it earlier, and I'll say it again: *Learn how to use your electronic gadgets.* Do not let a ringing phone, pager, Palm, or BlackBerry disturb others. Phone manufacturers have made this easier to do. Read the manual and learn how to do it!

3. *No Cell YELL.* People speak too loudly and disturb others. We don't need to hear one another's conversations. Some people believe, as one woman told me, "The louder I speak, the better I hear." That is not true! Remind yourself to speak in a quiet, conversational voice and lower your chin so your mouth is facing down. The volume carries less that way.

4. *Do not answer the phone in front of others.* Ellen was looking for a new home. The real estate agent was young, smart, and on the ball in most respects, but not when it came to the phone. She had the most up-to-date hands-free device, and the phone was permanently attached to her ear. She spent practically every moment on the phone talking with other clients and the home office. She *never* let a call go into voicemail. That was great for some clients, but finally Ellen got so frus-

trated by the interruptions in midsentence, she switched to another agent.

It's easy to fall into the cell-phone trap—that is, to answer a cell phone whenever it rings. Especially susceptible are those of us who, like the real estate agent, need to keep in frequent (if not, as she seemed to believe, constant) touch. As with the retro (tele)phone, answering the cell phone while others are present is simply rude. The agent was ignoring her client, and in this case, paid the ultimate price—she lost the client's business.

5. *Do not multitask.* Do not talk on the phone and write an email or conduct any other business at the same time. A dry-cleaner put up the following sign:

> WE WILL NO LONGER WAIT ON YOU IF YOU ARE ON YOUR CELL PHONE.
> PLEASE DO NOT ENTER THE STORE UNTIL YOU ARE FINISHED WITH
> YOUR CONVERSATION.

Four hundred people have asked him where he got the sign!

6. *Don't let them become a distraction.* Phones and other electronic gadgets aren't toys; do not play with them. Do not put your phone, your pager, your laptop, or your Palm on the desk in front of you. Don't check email, access the Internet, etc., unless it's appropriate to the meeting.

7. *Do not discuss private or confidential business in public.* You never know who may be nearby, and someone—your competition, for example—may hear you and learn information that can be helpful to them.

8. *Don't be rude to a cell-phone abuser.* You can politely ask someone to lower his or her voice or put his or her phone on

vibrate. Use the word *please* and explain the reason for your request. Put your request in the form of a question—"Could you please lower your voice? We can hear your whole conversation." It's a gentler way to assert yourself.

9. *Remove your headset when you are not using the phone.* It should not be permanently attached to your ear! And be prepared for others to comment on your conversation if you walk and talk into your headset at the same time. Kevin was sent to me by his company, a very large manufacturing firm, for coaching. Kevin was excellent at his job but the higher-ups felt he need some "executive polish" before he could move up in the organization. He arrived for the first session with a small headset wrapped around his ear. One of the first things we discussed was the need to remove the headset. It's not an earring!

10. *Select appropriate ring tones.* Keep it simple, make it something you can easily identify, and set the volume to an audible, but not blaring, level.

 Pachter's Pointer: Know the law and your company's policy.

In some states it is illegal to drive and use a phone unless it's hands-free. Your company may have rules of its own.

50. Top six things to do (or not do) in a meeting when a cell phone rings.

1. *Do not* sing along with the musical ring tone.

2. *Do not* yell, "For the love of all that is holy, turn your phone off!"

3. *Do not* say, "You know, it is really rude to answer your phone in front of me. Didn't your mother teach you any manners?" This is not the way to get someone's business!

4. *Do not* start to wiggle in the chair like a child looking for a bathroom pass in the hope that you will be allowed to leave the room. If it looks like it will be a long or personal conversation, nonverbally signal the person to see if you should wait outside.

5. *Do* take out a copy of my book *The Jerk with the Cell Phone: A Survival Guide for the Rest of Us* and start reading. Make sure the book is positioned so the person sees it. (A reader of the book said it works every time!)

6. *Do* leave your copy of the book behind, if the person continues to act like a jerk throughout the meeting.

 Pachter's Pointer: Whatever you're carrying— Palms, pagers, beepers, BlackBerries, laptops, and other interrupters . . .

1. Learn how to use them.

2. Do not disturb others.

3. Pay attention to the people around the room.

4. Do not allow alarms, bells, whistles to go off when others are present. Turn the sound off or, if possible, set them to vibrate.

Say It Succinctly: Effective Voicemail Messages

Quinn always left very long, detailed, and often complicated voicemail messages. Most callers tuned out and never listened to the entire message, leaving Quinn frustrated when his teammates asked him questions he'd answered via voicemail. "Didn't you listen to my voicemail message?" he'd growl. "Nooooo," was the usual response. "I listened to the beginning . . ."

What Went Wrong?

The purpose of voicemail is to provide essential information as quickly and clearly as possible. Quinn's messages were too long and people stopped paying attention. Say what you need to say in as few words as possible.

51. When leaving a voicemail message . . .

1. *State your name and phone number;* repeat it at the beginning *and* at the end of the message, and don't forget to say the numbers slowly. People don't like to replay the message to get the number. "Hi, it's me," is not enough information!

2. *Speak clearly and succinctly.*

3. *Eliminate phone tag.* Explain the reason for your call and provide enough information so that the person you are calling can respond even if you are not available to take the call. If it is

BLUNDER BUSTER

Nowhere does KISS (Keep It Short and Simple) apply more than when leaving voicemail messages. To avoid wordiness, write down what you want to say *before* you leave a voicemail message. After you record it, most systems allow you to play it back. Listen carefully to your message. Were you clear? Were you concise? If not, rerecord the message until you are.

something that must be discussed, suggest times when you will be available to talk.

Your Voicemail Message Says a Lot: Make Sure It Says You're a Pro

Frank, a consultant, was trying to reach Cheryl to inform her of a change in the location of their forthcoming meeting. Each time he called—and he tried many times over the course of two days—Cheryl wasn't there and he kept getting a recording saying her mailbox was full. Cheryl had hired Frank because she was having difficulty maintaining relationships with her clients. Frank now knew one reason why!

What Went Wrong?

Your mailbox shouldn't be so full that people can't leave messages. If you are away from the office, check your messages regularly. Act on the ones that need a response and delete those that you no longer need. If need be, increase the amount of space you have so you can receive more messages. It is unprofessional and frustrating for someone to call you and not be able to leave a message. It may cost you business, too.

▶ **QUICK TIP:** If you are going to be away for an extended period and unable to pick up messages regularly, change your message so that people will know not to expect an immediate response. You might also recommend that they leave messages only if it is urgent and, if possible, give the number of another person who might be of assistance in your absence.

52. Messages made easy

1. *Keep your message simple.* KISS applies to the message callers hear when they reach your voicemail. "You've reached the voicemail of Barbara Pachter. Please leave your name, number, and a message, and I will return your call as soon as possible," is usually sufficient. You may want to identify your company or your department. You may also wish to leave the number of an alternate contact for those who need immediate assistance.

2. *If you update your message* daily or even occasionally to let others know when you will be out of the office, make sure you update the message when you return. It sounds unprofessional (and makes you appear sloppy) to hear someone tell you that he will be out of the office till Wednesday and the caller gets the message on Thursday!

▶ **QUICK TIP:** These message pointers apply to email, too. Some email systems, even at large companies, have a limit on the amount of material email boxes can hold. Clean out your mailbox regularly. Also, if you use the "vacation" or "out-of-office" function, be sure to change it when you return.

 Pachter's Pointer: Phone FAQs.

The following questions are asked frequently:

I have caller ID. Is it okay to let my caller know that I know who is calling?

It is best not to. You may be wrong if you answer, "Hi, Tom," as John may be using Tom's phone. For those not accustomed to the technology—I know they are getting fewer and fewer, but there are some—it can catch them off guard and make them uncomfortable.

I often get flustered when I expect to get a person's voicemail and the person answers. How can I cover my embarrassment?

The best answer is to *always* be prepared to speak to the person. I should point out, it's really not good manners to call at an off time in order to avoid speaking to someone, but we all know it's a fairly common occurrence. Still, no matter when you call, you can never be certain the person won't answer. So take the Boy Scout motto to heart and "Be Prepared!"

I own a small business. Is it okay to use call-waiting in business?

No. It is rude to the person to whom you are talking. Instead of call-waiting, invest in a voicemail system that will answer the phone when the line is busy and allow other callers to leave messages. Then make certain you pick up your messages after you've finished your call, and, if needed, return the calls promptly.

Group Speak: Teleconferencing

During a weekly team teleconference, Carol called Anthony an idiot. The following week, she was due for her review and was looking forward to learning she'd been promoted. Her supervisor had hinted that it was almost a sure thing. To her surprise, the promotion was postponed.

What Went Wrong?

Name calling is not okay, whether in person or on the phone. Yet, because we don't see the other person, we sometimes say things we'd never say (and shouldn't ever say) in face-to-face talks. Certain things never change, and just because the technology is new, being rude is being rude, regardless of the medium.

53. Teleconferencing tips.

1. *Choose it for the right reasons.* Like email, teleconferencing can be very efficient and cost-effective if used appropriately. It's a great way to bring people from different locations together for sharing information. It is usually not as effective when you have to make a decision about something or work collectively to solve problems.

2. *Start with introductions.* Each participant should state his or her name, title, and location so everyone knows who is on the call.

3. *Distribute an agenda* before the meeting so participants can prepare for it.

4. *Use a strong meeting facilitator* to make sure that the agenda is followed. The facilitator also needs to make sure that everyone gets an opportunity to contribute. If there are several people in a room at one end of the line and a single individual or single individuals at various locations at the other end, it may be more difficult for those that are flying solo to jump in. The facilitator can make sure that everyone gets a chance to participate. I hear many complaints about teleconferencing— perhaps more than about any other form of new technology. I've found that often these problems could easily be solved if there were an experienced facilitator guiding the teleconference.

5. *Pay attention to your voice.* Speak clearly, succinctly, and loudly. Repeat your name before you start talking. Although you've introduced yourself at the beginning, not everyone will recognize your voice.

Pachter's Pointer: Learn how to use the equipment.

Sarah, a training manager, had her boss on the phone when she conference-called a consultant to discuss an upcoming program. The consultant was not in, so Sarah left a message. She then continued to talk with her boss about the consultant. What she didn't know was that she had not dropped the connection with the consultant, who heard the entire conversation when she retrieved her voicemail messages. Fortunately for Sarah, everything she said was complimentary.

6. *Close the door.* Conference calls can distract everyone within earshot, so remember to close the door before you begin. This is doubly important if the conversation is confidential.

▶ **QUICK TIP:** The same applies to conversations on speakerphones. If you are in your office and put your phone on speakerphone, it's polite to let the caller know who, if anyone, is in your office. It can be embarrassing if you don't. Also, only use your speakerphone when absolutely necessary. Most phones don't have the same sound quality when they are on speakerphone, which makes it harder for the listener.

A word to the wise about blogs . . .

One young woman, we'll call her Kate, wrote some horrible things about her boss and the company she worked for on her blog. She thought she was in the clear because she'd received and accepted an offer from another firm. Somehow—no one knows quite how—her prospective employer came across the blog and rescinded the offer.

The moral of this story is painfully clear: Never say anything in either techno or retro format that you wouldn't want the other person to hear. What you say can and will come back to haunt you.

Whatever you put on your website or blog, the rules of etiquette apply. From a strictly business point of view, ask yourself, "Do I really want my boss (or anyone you work with) to know *that* about *me*?" And, of course, don't bad-mouth anyone. It only makes you look bad and can make readers who know you wonder what you'll be saying about them.

Don't forget to keep the graphics and language professional—no X-rated photos, cursing, or profanities allowed. Once again, you may be writing with friends or like-minded web trawlers in mind, but the world may be watching, and you never know when you might meet an offended reader who turns out to be your next big client, future colleague, or potential boss. As with anything you write, proofread, proofread, proofread. No typos or spelling errors. Your blog (or website) is a picture of you—and you want that picture to be attractive and professional.

▶ **QUICK TIP:** Follow your company's guidelines on what you may or may not do on a blog. Most say you may not include any confidential or proprietary information. But policies vary from firm to firm, so it's wise to check before you blog. You don't want to get "dooced"—netspeak for losing your job or getting fired because of something you put on your blog or website. Don't assume you can remain anonymous; coworkers have been known to let their supervisors know about another employee's website.

PART FIVE

Your Career Is What You Make It: Business Skills to Take You Up the Corporate Ladder

Career development is a continuing process. You always want to create and take advantage of opportunities, get noticed, develop your skills, and establish relationships. As with everything else in business, there is a right and wrong way to do things, and perhaps nowhere in your life is etiquette more important than in building your career.

You may be the smartest and the best qualified for the job, but if you come across as rude, arrogant, or ineffective in your interactions with those in- and outside the office, it will reflect badly on your ability to work with or lead others. On the other hand, if you know how to carry yourself in any situation, speak and write well, and are considerate

Top Ten Career Killers

1. *Poor behavior.* Rudeness, lack of common courtesy, and inappropriate actions—words, deeds, even how you dress will be remembered. To get ahead, you want to be and be seen as a credible professional. How you act influences people's perception of you as much as (some say more than) how well you do your job.

2. *Un-likeability.* In a recent *USA Today* article, likeability was cited as key to advancement; it also pointed out that employees who were liked tended to get bigger raises than those who weren't.

3. *Unreliability.* If you say you are going to do something, do it. And do it on time—meet your deadlines. In fact, it helps to go that extra mile and lend a hand to a colleague when it's needed and to volunteer for extra assignments.

4. *Lack of a network.* To get ahead, it is essential to establish good relationships with people both up and down the corporate ladder. People tend to do business with people they know. Work at developing your network—you want to know and be known. Remember to do the "simple" things that mean a lot: greet people, shake hands, make small talk, and so on.

5. *Sloppy and inferior work.* This one is a no-brainer, isn't it? Quality counts. Pay attention to the details.

6. *Stagnation.* Professional development is vital to career success. Think strategically about your career and your goals. Take advantage of any training programs or opportunities for formal education that your company offers or provides reimbursement for. Keep yourself up to date on what's happening in your profession by reading trade publications and attending association meetings, if possible. Also, keep abreast of applicable technology. Find mentors and be on the lookout for role models. Ask for and accept feedback.

7. *Inappropriate attire.* This applies, of course, to your position and to your company's culture, and extends to the event you are attending. In

business, you want to be taken seriously, and what you wear can either enhance people's opinions of your professionalism or detract from it.

8. *Poor communication skills.* The information you impart—verbally and non-verbally—says a great deal about you and contributes to how people view you. You send a message—and not a positive one—if, for example, you don't look at people when you speak to them or don't listen when they speak, if you interrupt frequently, or use poor diction. Conversely, if you speak loudly enough to be heard, make effective presentations, write well, and speak well of yourself without being pushy or arrogant, the message you send will signal your competence and professionalism.

9. *Inability to handle conflict.* In our work lives, as in our personal lives, there are people with whom we disagree. As a business professional, it is important to learn how to confront people when necessary. Gossiping, bad-mouthing, or complaining about colleagues and co-workers is definitely off limits, as are cursing and yelling.

10. *Lack of social skills.* Out-of-the-office interactions are more important than many people think. Not socializing with others, poor table manners, arriving late, all work against your image as a professional. Do not think that you can let it all hang out just because you are out of the office. Jobs have been lost and careers ruined because a person drank too much, or said or did something ridiculous at a corporate function.

and tactful, the odds are that your move up the corporate ladder will be enhanced.

To get ahead in today's competitive environment, you want your colleagues and others to think of you as *the* credible source— someone who cares about his career, knows her job, understands the work environment and the people in it, and presents herself to others in a professional manner.

You don't have to be a "brown nose" or "yes" man or woman to get ahead, but, in addition to having "smarts," you do have to mind those proverbial Ps and Qs to advance in today's competitive corporate environment.

Use Your Head to Get Ahead

A large manufacturer was submitting a proposal for a huge amount of work to FedEx. The final proposal—with all the Is dotted and Ts crossed, checked and triple checked—was given to the director's secretary, Caroline, who was told to get it delivered to FedEx, which she did. So what's the problem? Would you believe Caroline UPS'd the proposal!

No surprise, the manufacturer did not get the contract! When the director followed up with FedEx to find out what was wrong with the proposal, he was told it had nothing to do with the proposal—only the mode of delivery. Enraged, the director stormed into Caroline's office, demanding an explanation. Surprised, she sputtered, "I just didn't think about it. We *always* use UPS." She resigned soon after.

What Went Wrong?

Duh! It's pretty obvious, isn't? Caroline was doing her job; she got the package out promptly, but she wasn't thinking about what was in it or where it was going. She was not thinking about what impact her actions would have on the work, the relationship, the client, or potential client.

"But we always . . ." doesn't always work. We get comfortable doing things one way; we like our routine, and don't think what it could mean to those on the receiving end. As in Caroline's case, thoughtlessness can be costly.

54. Consider the consequences.

1. *It pays to think before you act.* I believe your behavior matters, but will it *always* matter? No. Will it occasionally matter? Yes. Will it sometimes be *the* deciding factor in whether you get the client, customer, promotion, or establish the relationship? You bet your life. So is it worth using your head all the time? I think so.

   From the littlest task to the biggest project, it's obvious that everything we do has an impact. Whether you are stuffing envelopes or writing a multimillion-dollar proposal, everything can have consequences and doing things well counts.

2. *Remember, what goes around comes around.*

   Calvin, now the manager of a warehouse, told me that early in his career he had made it his "personal mission to make life miserable" for one of his employees. That employee later became his boss and, eventually, when the timing was right, let Calvin go.

   Behaving badly to others usually comes back to haunt you and damage your career. Calvin learned the lesson in just about the hardest way possible. It sounds too simplistic yet the old adage, "Be nice to people on the way up because you may see them on the way down," is still true. And why be nasty, anyway?

3. *Ask yourself, How will my action affect others?* For example, will sending a thank-you note impress a client? Will common courtesy—*all* the time—to mailroom staff gain their support when you've got a rush project that must get to the post office on a Friday afternoon? Will a smile and a hello make life more pleasant for everyone I meet? The answer to these questions is

obvious, but when we're harried, we don't always remember to do these things, and we should.

55. More ways to use your head to get ahead . . .

- *Expand your capabilities.* Learn new things. Read. Know your field. Stay up to date. Take advantage of the training that your company provides. Go back to school; get that degree or take a class. Not only will you develop yourself, but you will also expand your *network.*

- *Do good work and work hard.* Do what you say you will do, meet your deadlines, and whenever you can, go above and beyond.

- *Find a mentor/be a mentor.* Mentors take an active role in your career development and can help guide you as you advance in your field. Take advantage of your company's mentoring program if there is one, or use your own network to find someone to work with you.

- *Have role models.* Role models may or may not be people you know personally. They can be alive or dead. They don't have an active role in your career development, but you learn from watching them or reading or hearing about their experiences and how they conducted themselves. They may make things seem possible: If they could do it, you can, too.

Come Blow Your Horn

Discussing his management style at an introductory meeting, Sal, a new manager, told his staff, "I don't want to tell anyone how to do his or her job." Sheila raised her hand and said, "I don't know. I would like someone to tell me how to do my job." Sal responded, "If you don't know how to do your job, why are you in this position?"

What Went Wrong?

First and foremost, it's important not to put yourself down or seem to be putting yourself down. Yes, she was trying to be humorous, but she was putting herself down in her new boss's (and perhaps in her co-workers') eyes; potentially destroying his (and their) confidence in her. Learning when and how to speak well of yourself is an important step to getting and staying ahead. Because if you don't, who will?

Tactful self-promotion is an essential business skill, and the art of self-promotion is a far cry from bragging. Most of us find braggarts obnoxious—definitely not a good move if you want to get ahead. On the other hand, shrinking violets don't move ahead either. The key is to let people know your good qualities and accomplishments without overdoing it. Good work alone won't do it, but there are ways to get the message across.

56. Master the fine art of self-promotion.

1. *Be prepared.* You may often find yourself in situations where you have to tell others about yourself; for example, when you

join a group or introduce yourself at a meeting. For times like these, it always pays to have prepared a line or two, such as, "I'm Tom Smith, the new director of sales. Joan Jones brought me in to start the new field service project," which will allow you to speak comfortably about yourself and your accomplishments.

2. *Accept compliments graciously.* People tend to be uncomfortable when they are complimented, and so they minimize their achievements. A very capable woman I know, when congratulated by the president of her division on landing a big account, responded "Oh *that*—no big deal." When you deny or make little of a compliment you are putting yourself down and, in a sense, insulting the person who gave you the compliment.

Please do remember that humor can backfire: One vice president, after receiving a Woman of the Year award, said "I don't know why they chose me. Where are their standards?" She was trying to be funny, but the joke bombed with the audience there to honor her.

BLUNDER BUSTER

If you have difficulty accepting compliments, train yourself to say "Thank you," and then shut your mouth!

If you are able, try adding a few words after saying thank you that build on the compliment:

"I really appreciate that."

"I enjoyed working on it."

"It was a wonderful challenge."

"I worked hard on that project. Your words mean a lot to me."

3. *When asked, do tell.* If someone says, "How are things at work?" this is your opportunity to talk about your accomplishments. And it's important to express genuine pleasure when you do. When I was asked that question recently I said, "I have great news. I was just interviewed by a national business magazine!"

 Pachter's Pointer: Keep a record of your accomplishments.

> Write down what you have accomplished. If you don't, you may overlook specific achievements when you update your résumé, discuss your successes during your performance review, or prepare for an interview.

4. *Avoid superlatives,* such as "I felt like the greatest . . ." Instead, simply describe what you did, such as, "Using the new numbers from our field offices, I was able to cut our costs by a quarter."

5. *Use comparisons that reflect positively on you.* A director I coached had run the Boston Marathon. I suggested she use her experience preparing for the marathon as a way to answer questions about how she would prepare for a company's market expansion. Naturally, the higher-ups were quite impressed by the fact that she had run the marathon, and could easily see how that dedication could translate into on-the-job success.

6. *Weave your accomplishments into the conversation, when appropriate.* I use my experiences to illustrate key teaching points in my classes and seminars. In doing so, I highlight my accomplishments. For example, when discussing how important it is to prepare for an overseas assignment, I talk about the things

I did before I spoke at a groundbreaking women's seminar in Kuwait.

7. *Don't talk about yourself all the time or the same accomplishment over and over.* It will make you sound like a braggart or a bore, and you don't want to be either. The key is to achieve a balance. It's important to speak of other things.

8. *Speak well of others.* This is a gracious act and is usually appreciated by the other person. Plus, when you praise others, your comments about yourself don't seem unusual. (Of course don't praise someone if it isn't warranted. People know and will brand you as a phony.)

Make the Most of Meetings

Katie, a salesperson, hid her new kitten in a large briefcase and brought it to a meeting with customers. She thought no one would notice. They didn't, until it started to purr loudly. It was rather funny at the time, but Katie didn't get the sale. Her customers were so distracted by the interruption, they could not remember much of what Katie had said about the product.

What Went Wrong?

Why would anybody do this? Anything you do that can take attention away from your message will diminish your professional image. I know, most people don't take kittens to work and certainly not to meetings, but the point is that it's easy to distract people from your message by doing little things such as fidgeting (see Part Three), chewing gum, not being prepared, allowing your cell phone to ring, or worse, taking calls.

57. Six ways to make meetings work.

1. *Arrive on time.* Go up to people and greet any other attendees who have arrived. Shake hands correctly and make small talk. These "little" things will help you, and others, feel part of the group.

2. *Prepare.* Know what will be discussed and who will be attending. Think about what you might add to the discussion and prepare what you will say about topics you may wish to raise.

BLUNDER BUSTER

There's no real way to recover when you get caught trying to get away with something other than to apologize, and occasionally, humor can help. Katie might have recovered if she apologized for the disruption and made a small joke—"Oops, the cat's out of the bag!" But if the cat had continued to cause a distraction, she would have had to leave the meeting. Not a good thing for her— or your—career!

Anticipate any objections and how you will respond to them. Think about what you will say when other topics come up. If those topics aren't brought up, you haven't lost anything. If they are, you are prepared.

Pachter's Pointer: If you are nervous about speaking up . . .

Speak early in the meeting. The longer you wait, the harder it will be.

3. *Pay attention.* Sit still. Listen as others speak. No doodling. Do not use your Palm Pilot, BlackBerry, computer, or cell phone, including text messaging, during the meeting—unless its use is part of the meeting. Limit side discussions.

4. *Take notes judiciously.* It is possible to take too many notes. You can distract yourself and those around you. Those who don't know you might think you were the secretary rather than a participant or, as one man I coached was surprised to learn, people thought he was taking notes in order to reprimand subordinates later.

BLUNDER BUSTER

It's easy to avoid problems if you plan ahead and follow a few simple rules.

If you are running the meeting . . .

- Prepare an agenda.

- Send out material in advance.

- Make sure the room is ready for the meeting.

- Set meeting guidelines and schedule breaks if the meeting is going to be long.

- Keep people focused and on track—"That's a good point; now, let's get back to the agenda."

- Stand as you get the meeting started, if it's a formal meeting.

- Send out a summary or minutes of the meeting, when appropriate.

When the meeting's in someone's office . . .

- Knock if the door is closed, or announce your arrival.

- Ask if the person is ready or, if it is an impromptu meeting, ask if it is a convenient time.

- If the person is on the phone, do not walk in. Nonverbally signal that you will be outside or you will come back.

5. *Learn the table.* Is the agenda followed? Does the meeting start on time? Do you have to arrive early to get a good seat? Do people wait their turns to speak or are interruptions okay? Generally you want to avoid interrupting others (more on

interruptions in the next section), but some meetings are free-for-alls. People just jump in at any time and talk over one another. If that's the case, if you don't jump in and interrupt, you may never be heard.

6. *Follow up on any commitments you made.* Lack of follow-through negatively affects your professional reputation.

"Excuse Me!": Interrupting

Craig was speaking to a customer, explaining the advantages of the latest software program when his colleague Jeannette chimed in with, "And did you know that it also can . . ." She went on and on. The first time it happened, Craig waited until Jeannette finally stopped talking and then continued explaining the features. Soon, Jeannette piped up again; Craig tried to continue but Jeannette kept on until finally the customer said, "Hey! Let the guy finish!"

What Went Wrong?

It's a fact; people don't like to be interrupted! It's rarely necessary that you (or anyone else, for that matter) have something so important to say that it merits interrupting the person who is speaking.

Interrupting, as we've said, can be particularly difficult at meetings when one (or more) of the attendees feels he or she has to chime in although the speaker is in mid-sentence. Hold your comments until the person has finished talking or, as happened to one up-and-coming young executive, you may be asked not to attend—at least until you've learned to hold your tongue.

When you interrupt you can seem inconsiderate, abrasive, and, worse, aggressive—even if you are trying to be helpful. Interrupting is an annoying habit and your professional image will suffer if you don't break the habit. Often, an interrupter is unaware of his or her behavior, but that's no excuse.

Three Signs That You May Be an Interrupter

1. You catch yourself mouthing the words that you think the other person is going to say.

2. You finish the speaker's sentences just to move the conversation along.

3. A trusted friend or colleague confirms that you interrupt too much.

58. How to break the interrupting habit.

1. *Acknowledge it.* Tell yourself that you really do interrupt and that interrupting is a habit you want to break.

2. *Jot down reminders,* if possible. If someone says something that you want to comment on, instead of immediately cutting in, listen and write down the key words—only the key words. Wait until the person has finished speaking and then make your comment.

3. *Before speaking, question yourself.* In a one-on-one conversation, ask yourself: "Have I given the other person a chance to finish speaking?" or, "Is my comment necessary? What will it add to the conversation?"

It may take some time to break the interrupting habit, but if you are aware of it, you can do it.

59. What to do if you're interrupted.

1. *Be gracious.* Remember that occasional interruptions do occur. Responding rudely will hurt your credibility. And if it's your CEO who is interrupting you, let him or her do it!

2. *Continue speaking.* The interrupter should get the hint.

3. *Try a polite, but powerful response,* such as:
   "I'll discuss that as soon as I am finished."
   "I'll be happy to address that as soon as I finish my thought."
   "Hold that thought."
   "Excuse me, I wasn't finished."

Say it in a neutral, not a harsh, tone of voice.

"It Won't Play in Peoria!": Interfering with Someone's Job

After a long and brutal job search, Conner started working for a financial consulting firm. His best friend, who worked at an advertising agency, wanted to make it a memorable first day so he sent a clown with a large bouquet of balloons to Conner's new office. He thought it would be a fun way to break the ice with his buddy's new colleagues. Conner was mortified. As his worst nightmare unfolded, all Conner could do was pray that his colleagues would succumb to a severe case of collective amnesia. Of course, they didn't! It took a while for the clown jokes to end.

What Went Wrong?

You can't have fun, entertain, or play jokes in someone else's workplace. It's absolutely off limits. You are playing with someone's livelihood, and, since you can't be sure what can cause a problem or embarrass the other person, it's too dangerous.

60. A job is not a joking matter.

1. *Be conservative.* If you want to send a gift to someone's workplace, play it safe. Yes, it may be boring, a plant doesn't have a red nose or wear floppy shoes—but as Conner would tell you, that's ever so much better!

2. *No practical jokes.* It's just not funny. I remember seeing a TV show where a man's presentation was switched by his

colleagues. Instead of a slide showing his research, it showed the man in a bathing suit at a swimming pool. The audience was confused; the man was mortified.

3. *Every company is different* and different companies have different corporate environments. What may be acceptable in one company may be quite unacceptable at another. If you do not work there, you cannot know where the line is. Don't assume that what you are doing will be okay.

"Kvetch, Kvetch, Kvetch": Negativity at Work

Aida was up for promotion. Her work was excellent, but at the promotion committee meeting, one colleague said, "I avoid her as much as I can. She is always complaining about something." Aida didn't get the promotion.

What Went Wrong?

Stop complaining! Complaining is draining and incredibly negative. People get tired of listening to the same negative comments about someone or something over and over and over.

If you are feeling negative about something, don't let those feelings show on the job. It can be a career killer. Who wants to be around someone who complains, puts people down, often disagrees with you, or generally talks about downbeat topics? No one does.

Negative people don't get the promotions, the awards, the great references, or the plum projects. Sad but true, these lost opportunities in turn increase their negativity. It becomes an endless cycle of disappointment and unhappiness at work.

61. How to be a more positive professional.

1. *Avoid downbeat topics.* Don't discuss negative things. You don't want to keep talking about how you lost the contract, how bad the economy is, and so on. Learn from your mistakes, accept your limitations, and move on.

BLUNDER BUSTER

Tie a string around your finger . . .
If you tend toward negativity, put a small sign on your desk with the letters K-I-P (Keep It Positive). Or arrange some sort of signal with a close colleague; for example, one manager would pass a note to his direct report with a coded message, B+ (be positive), if he become negative in meetings.

2. *Disagree agreeably.* If you say, "You're wrong," or, "You blew it," you're usually perceived to be on the attack, even when you're right. Instead say, "I see it differently," or, "I disagree." These statements demonstrate respect for the other person, and are not dismissive.

3. *Don't talk negatively about others.* Constantly criticizing others makes you look bad. If you have an issue with someone, talk to the person, and try to resolve it. If you are uncomfortable confronting others, see Part Six on conflict resolution.

4. *Correct other people only when necessary.* If a colleague says, "It took us twenty minutes to do something," is it crucial that you comment, "Well, actually it was twenty-five minutes"? If it's not important, why say anything? If you do it frequently, you may come across as fault-finder or nitpicker or, worse, as someone who likes to make others look bad.

5. *Accentuate the positive.* One manager said, "I don't want my people viewed as unprofessional or incompetent." Another put it this way: "I want my people viewed as professional and

competent." Which would you rather hear? The positive spin, of course; who wouldn't?

6. *No gloomy stares.* Maintain a pleasant facial expression.

 Pachter's Pointer: Fake it till you feel it.

If you are not a naturally positive person, don't worry. Simply start acting like one. Eventually, you'll find yourself becoming more positive.

Common Courtesy
Should be Common Sense

Fran, a young woman, asked her manager, Adam, to put in a good word for her with the director of the division. Adam did it and she got the promotion. Fran never thanked him. The manager never went out of his way for Fran again. And it was costly. A few months later, when asked for his opinion of her for a special assignment, Adam stayed quiet.

What Went Wrong?

Fran did not acknowledge the help she received. Not only is this downright rude in any circumstance, it is downright dumb in business. Little things like saying please and thank you—for things large and small, and putting a good word in with the director is large—help grease the wheels of business relationships. They make life run smoothly. When they're forgotten, they can become little or big irritants and can work against you as you try to advance. People remember those who are thoughtful; they also remember those who aren't. Had Adam said something positive, Fran undoubtedly would've gotten the assignment. Her lack of courtesy cost her Adam's support.

62. You catch more flies with honey.

1. *Be polite.* Say please, thank you, you're welcome, I appreciate that.

Instead of

"Get this to me by 3 p.m."

say

"Please get this to me by 3 p.m."

You'll see the difference. Not long ago, I was practicing a speech in which I spoke about the need for polite language in front of my then eleven-year-old son, Jake. His comment says a great deal: "Mom, you tell me to say please and thank you. Why do you need to tell adults?" I can't be the only mom telling her child to use polite language. Somewhere between childhood and adulthood we stop using these words. We need to remember to use them.

2. *Write thank-you notes.* Not only do you need to say thank you, you also need to write notes. If someone helps you or goes out of their way for you, send a note. It's a great way, and sometimes a required way, to acknowledge someone's assistance (see Part Two for more on thank-you notes).

3. *Help others.* When you can, why not help others? Tomorrow you may be the one who needs help. Of course that shouldn't be the only reason: Business is a team effort, and for a team to run smoothly and work to get done efficiently, you must all pull together for the good of all.

4. *Be considerate when sharing space with others.* Whether it's a conference room, cubicle, office, or equipment that's being shared, what you do affects others. Therefore:

   - *Do not* speak loudly on the phone, wear strong perfume, or play loud music.

- *Do* return anything you borrow.

- *Do* clean up after yourself; make certain to throw away empty coffee cups or trash.

- *Do* fix or let people know that something is broken.

- *Do* follow the guidelines. If you need to sign up in advance for a class, conference room, or shared equipment, do so.

- *Do* let someone go ahead of you, if you are copying a number of items or a lengthy document and that person has just one copy to make.

5. *Don't snoop.* Ruth, a salesperson, was left alone in her client's office when the client had to leave for a moment. Jane, the man's secretary, walked in on Ruth as she was looking through the customer's desk. She hoped to find out who her competition was. She not only was asked to leave, but a call was made to Ruth's employer. What Ruth was doing was akin to stealing.

   Even if you're not seeking information on the competition and are "just a little curious" or bored, keep your hands and your eyes off the information on anyone else's desk and computer screen. It's simply none of your business.

6. *Be dignified.* No practical jokes. This is the office, not the schoolyard. You can embarrass people. No drama either—it's rude and it usually backfires. One woman stood up dramatically in a meeting and announced, "I'm quitting," and stormed off. She could never ask that boss for a reference!

7. *Do not put people down.* You do not build yourself up by putting others down; in fact, you usually just look bad. This actually happened to a supervisor named Sean, who attended one of my classes. At the time he was a new supervisor, and was meeting with his new group. During the introductions, he noticed that one member of his team had still not arrived, and wondered aloud what had happened to him. Morgan, another member of the group, blurted out, "We all have a problem with him; he's never on time for meetings." Sean told me he squelched Morgan with, "Let me find that out for myself."

This rule applies to your competition as well. It will leave clients and potential clients wondering what you might say about them. Inappropriate comments about another company to clients generally reflect negatively on you and your company. If a client asks you to compare yourself to your competitor, talk about the merits of the product your firm offers, the great price, the customer service; forget about saying the competition are all cheap imitations and lazy bums who'd try to sell you the Brooklyn Bridge if they could. It can cost you the account.

8. *Show respect for everyone.* One man's administrative assistant heard him refer to her as, "She's just the admin." She never went out of her way for him again.

Which One Are You?

As you move up the corporate ladder you will find yourself managing others. Knowing how to communicate successfully with your employees is key to your career success.

Everyone falls somewhere along the spectrum of *too nice, too tough*, or *just right*. You probably won't identify with all of the characteristics of any one style—just keep working toward a middle ground.

TOO NICE	TOO TOUGH	JUST RIGHT
You're overly friendly with your employees, and as a result, they don't take you as seriously as they should.	You are not at all friendly with your employees and seldom socialize or make small talk with them. You rarely bother to say hello or goodbye.	You are polite—you don't yell or swear. You greet and acknowledge your employees and make occasional small talk with them.
You find it difficult to reprimand others when their performance is unacceptable. Therefore, you put it off, sugarcoat it, or pretend there's no problem.	You're incredibly demanding, and people shy away from you.	You're powerful—you get the job done. You don't love conflict, but you know how to handle and resolve it.
Since you're so friendly, you have to ask again and again to get things done. Your employees know they can get away with giving you excuses.	You don't praise employees when they do well (you believe it's their job), and problems can go unresolved because your employees won't talk to you or tell you the truth.	You give specific instructions and hold your employees accountable when they don't perform—and you recognize them when they do. You are available to your employees and spend some time getting to know them.

TOO NICE	TOO TOUGH	JUST RIGHT
Too Nice managers smile too much, beat around the bush, use passive language, and apologize for things that aren't their fault or don't warrant an apology—e.g., "I'm so sorry that you had a difficult time with the project."	The *Too Tough* ones speak loudly and curse when angry. They sometimes yell or use phrases such as, "Find a way to do it, damn it!" or, "Just get it done. Understand?" They rarely smile and often interrupt others. They have a tendency to point at others when speaking.	*Just Right*'s body language is relaxed yet strong. They don't wring their hands or play with things while others are speaking. They are not wishy-washy with their language and will use direct statements when appropriate, such as, "I need this by 3 p.m.," or, "The presentation needs improvement in the following areas . . ."

Walking a Tightrope: The Office Romance

June screamed and yelled at her boyfriend, whose office was in the neighboring cubicle. Everyone in the room heard much more than they wanted to know about how he had cheated on her with her best friend as well as all the other sordid details of this romance gone very sour!

What Went Wrong?

It's easy to say, "Don't do it," but we all know it happens. Still, you run a great risk when you date someone who works for the same company, especially if you're in the same office. If the relationship ends, regardless of the reason, you may have to face the person regularly, which can be painful, or at least uncomfortable. Should this happen, and we all know it does, be grown up about it. No scenes—no matter what has happened—in the office.

63. How to handle the office dating game.

1. *Don't date your boss.* If you just can't help yourselves, have your reporting relationship changed.

2. *No romantic displays.* No hand holding, hugging, kissing, or any other romantic display in the office. This also means no sexy emails and no Valentine's Day or other cards at work.

All presents, candy, and flowers should be delivered to your home.

3. *Don't let your relationship interfere with your work.* Behave professionally: no four-hour lunches, no playing favorites.

"Make Yourself Comfortable": Making Visitors Feel Wanted

Kimberly sat patiently in the reception area, looking at brochures and waiting for Sonia, the interviewer with whom she had an appointment. Ten, fifteen, twenty minutes passed and still no Sonia. The receptionist smiled, but nothing happened. He didn't call Sonia again or offer any explanation. After thirty-five minutes, Kimberly said goodbye to the receptionist and left. The next day, she interviewed and received a job offer from a rival firm. Sonia's company lost a potentially great employee.

What Went Wrong?

Emergencies do arise, and Sonia may not have been able to meet Kimberly at the appointed time; but she should have come out personally and apologized and offered an explanation, told Kimberly how long she anticipated she would be, asked if she wanted coffee, water, a soft drink, and offered to reschedule if that was more convenient. If, for some reason, Sonia could not personally do this, she should have gotten word to the receptionist, who should have done these things.

64. Lay out the welcome mat.

1. *Meet visitors and escort them to your office.* As we've said, you or an associate can do this. Do not keep people waiting. If you are unexpectedly tied up, get a message to the person,

Make a PACT
For More Effective Customer Etiquette

I designed the Make a PACT model to help employees use their etiquette skills to enhance customer relations, but, because customers are internal as well as external, it can be used in a wide variety of business situations. Each letter in PACT stands for a key action that should occur between a company representative and the customer.

- *Present yourself well.* Use open body language, wear a pleasant facial expression, make eye contact, dress appropriately.

- *Acknowledge the customer.* Be proactive, use a greeting, shake hands correctly, use the person's name when you can.

- *Connect with the customer.* Listen, make small talk, give accurate information, solve problems, deliver on your promises.

- *Thank the customer.* Say "goodbye" with an exit line that conveys your thanks and appreciation.

Use PACT every time, with every customer. Your last customer of the day should get the same level of professionalism as your first customer.

▶ **QUICK TIP:** PACT can also be used in your personal life; for example, when you meet new people or interact with a charity, board, or club member.

apologizing and explaining that you are running late and letting your guest know when you will be available.

2. *Greet your guest and shake hands.* Take the person's coat, and offer coffee, tea, or water, if they are available.

3. *Make introductions* to anybody else in the room that your visitor might not know. Let your guest know where to sit.

4. *Begin with a little small talk.* Get to know the person, then conduct your business. Make sure you listen carefully.

5. *End with goodbye* and escort, or have someone escort, the person out.

The #1 Fear: Stage Fright

Nicholas always became very nervous before making any presentation, large or small. He mentioned his severe attacks of stage fright to a friend, who recommended that he try one of her anti-anxiety drugs to help calm him down. He took one hoping it would help. It worked! That is, he wasn't nervous, but he spoke so slowly the audience wanted to run for the hills.

What Went Wrong?

"Make sure you have finished speaking before your audience has finished listening," said Dorothy Sarnoff, a noted speech consultant and author of *Never Be Nervous Again*. As someone who earns her living speaking to audiences large and small, I can attest to what good advice that is.

Throughout your career, you may be asked to make presentations. Whether you are providing information to your department or updating senior management on the status of a project, you want to effectively get your point across. Not only does the audience gain information, effective presentations make you look good—they're definitely a career booster!

65. How to avoid "presentation panic."

1. *Prepare and practice.* Of course you are going to be nervous if you don't prepare or practice your presentation.

- *Create notes of key phrases.* Be brief, but specific. Write enough so you can remember the whole thought. I recommend letter-size paper; note cards are too small.

- *Rehearse your talk using your notes.* Don't try to memorize your entire presentation word for word, because if you forget a word you will panic.

 Pachter's Pointer: Create a story file.

Stories bring your presentation to life. People remember the stories. But how do you get them so you have them when you go to prepare your speech? The answer is to create a story file. If you read about someone or experience something that is relevant to your area of expertise, tear it out or write it down and put it in a file. When you go to prepare your speech, look in the file; there will usually be stories you can use.

- *Number your pages.* It makes sense and it's very simple to do, yet people often forget to do this. Think about it: What would happen if you dropped your notes? Numbered, it's not a problem; unnumbered, it can be a nightmare.

- *Double space your text* and use a large easy-to-read font.

- *Practice out loud.* You want to hear how the words sound.

- *Time yourself.* Get a sense of your timing. And be prepared: Mark sections in your notes that can easily be eliminated if

The Q&A Challenge

If there is a Q&A scheduled, prepare by asking yourself what questions might be asked and decide how you will answer them. This is especially important for the tough questions. You don't want to be caught off guard.

- If there was no way you could have prepared for a particular question, or if you simply failed to anticipate it and don't have an answer, you can usually say, "I don't know, but I'll find out and get back to you."

- You will want your answers to appear spontaneous, so you don't want to keep referring to your notes (except to reference a specific point) when answering the questions.

- When you are asked a question, repeat it *before* you answer it. This gives you a little time to get your thoughts together and to paraphrase the question, which will also allow you to eliminate negativity, if any.

- Look at the audience when answering the question.

your time is cut short; also, box extra material that you can add during the presentation if you are running short or if you've been asked to stretch your presentation (for example, if the next speaker is late).

2. *Banish negative thoughts.* Think positively and say things that build your confidence. I say, before every presentation, "I can do it. I can handle this." It is part of my mental preparation. Remember, what you say *must* be positive. "I will not blow the presentation" is *not* positive.

3. *See it.* "To control my pre-race butterflies, I visualize each turn in the track," says NASCAR driver Jimmie Johnson. Visualization is used by many people, especially athletes, to calm their nerves. Visualize yourself giving the presentation you want to give. See yourself in the room succeeding!

 Pachter's Pointer: Ask yourself . . .

Does the audience know I am nervous?

If you don't give it away—verbally or nonverbally—your audience will *never* know. And if they don't know, why should you be nervous?

Where to Put Your Hands and Other Secrets of Powerful Presentations

Marco, a marketing executive, was concerned about his upcoming brand report to the top brass. He knew the brand had done well, but he dreaded giving the thirty-minute presentation. He prepared and practiced and felt he had done a good job. Still, the first person he met after the presentation said to him, "Nice presentation, but how come you kept your hands in your pockets the whole time?"

What Went Wrong?

It's a hand thing! We want to see people's hands. Marco's lack of gestures took away from his delivery. Keeping his hands in his pockets disturbed the audience, who wanted him to be more animated.

Gestures are important. They bring your words to life. But, like everything else, you can overdo them, too, which leads the audience to watch your movements and miss your message. When making a presentation, it's more important than ever to avoid nervous gestures such as wringing your hands, playing with a pen, or tapping on the podium. In addition to being a distraction, they tell people that you are nervous, which makes you appear less professional.

Pachter's Pointer: A picture is worth a thousand words.

A lovely woman told me she discovered that she giggled when she gave a talk, as she watched her identical twin sister giggle as she gave a talk. Since most of us don't have an identical twin to learn from, have yourself videotaped so that you can see what you are doing when you give a presentation. I know most of us hate looking at ourselves, but it is a great way to see what you do well and what could use improvement.

66. How to present like a pro.

1. *Pay attention to your posture.* Good posture helps convey confidence. Walk around a little if you can.

2. *Look at the people in the audience.* It helps you connect with them.

3. *Do not read your speech.* You don't want to look like a "bobble doll," with its head going up and down. It's okay to glance at your notes occasionally, but remember it's hard to connect with the audience if you end up just reading to them.

4. *Speak up, but don't yell.* A microphone will only carry your soft volume to the back of the room.

5. *Use easy-to-understand words.* When a speaker uses unfamiliar words, people often stop listening.

 Pachter's Pointer: What to wear when you are the presenter.

A general guideline is to dress *one level above the level of your audience.* You want to create an aura of credibility, and what you wear can help you achieve that image.

Seeing Is Believing: Visual Aids

Cecily was giving a presentation on "Best Practices," but her title slide in big, bold letters read: **"Beast Practices."** The audience laughed when they saw the slide. Cecily, who never turned to look at the slide, was confused and stumbled her way through the presentation.

What Went Wrong?

The slide was not proofed effectively. Your slide needs to be perfect. No mistakes.

BLUNDER BUSTER

Don't get flustered when you make a mistake. Cecily should have looked around to see what had caused the laughter. Once she understood what had happened, she could either have acknowledged it or made a joke of it and continued with the rest of her presentation. It was a mistake, it wasn't a tragedy.

67. Three ways to make your presentation visually inviting.

1. *Use visual aids to enhance your presentation.* Use visuals to *supplement* and *support* your presentation. Except in rare circumstances, they are not a substitute for your talk, and you don't want them to take attention away from you, the speaker.

2. *Don't turn your slides into eye charts!* I can't number the times I've heard someone say, "I know you can't read this one but it shows . . ." Make sure the audience can read the slide. Use a large, readable font. General guideline: Each slide should have a title followed by bulleted items.

3. *Talk to the audience, not the slide.* Speakers often turn their backs on the audience as they read the slide. Check to be certain that the correct slide is on the screen, and then turn back to the audience.

Networking Is Not Just for Computers: Develop and Nurture Yours

While at the opening reception of a conference, Karen went off into a corner, fired up her laptop, and proceeded to work. Her boss walked in and saw her. Needless to say, he was not pleased. "We spend several hundred dollars a year for you to be a member of this group," he told her. "These networking events are for you to meet people, *not* a place for you to be sitting in the corner by yourself. If you don't want to be here, there are others who do."

What Went Wrong?

Karen wasted an important (and expensive) opportunity. Networking is about making connections and forming valuable relationships. Networking is important in all areas—not just in business. And networking is a two-way street that can help you and the people with whom you network. It's an essential business activity, not a throwaway event or even an optional one. Don't blow the chance to meet new contacts, reconnect with colleagues, gain information about your company, or learn the latest buzz in your industry.

68. Network-building techniques.

1. *Get involved.* Join professional associations, attend meetings, and volunteer for committees. You will find out what is happening in your field, and you will meet new people to add to your network.

2. *Diversify.* Include people from other professions at different levels in your network. As Harvey MacKay wisely said in *Dig Your Well Before You're Thirsty*, "If everyone in your network is the same, it isn't a network, it's an anthill."

3. *Be a joiner.* Join company-sponsored teams, clubs, and activities. It's a way to meet people *and* have fun. But remember you don't want to develop a reputation as a "bad sport" or a "sore loser," so if sports are not your thing, remember that it's important to keep those negative emotions in check.

   A woman in my seminar told me that she had cursed out the catcher on her company's baseball team because he wasn't playing well. She didn't anticipate that six months later he would be interviewing her for a promotion. She didn't get the job.

4. *Stay in touch.* It's not enough to meet people or have a network; you need to nurture the relationships. Arrange an occasional lunch, send an email, send holiday cards, or make a call.

 Pachter's Pointer: Add a personal touch . . .

When sending holiday cards with your name imprinted, make sure you hand-sign them, and, when you can, add a short note.

5. *Follow through on commitments you make.* If you promised to send a copy of an article or share certain information, do it and do it promptly. It will be appreciated and remembered.

6. *Help others.* What goes around really does come around. When possible, be a resource to your coworkers. If you're aware of opportunities your colleagues could benefit from, let them know. Introduce people to others who may be able to help them.

Your Future Is Now: The Job Search

Lucas was eager for a promotion and new challenges, but did not want to leave his current firm. The environment was interesting, the people great to work with, and the location couldn't have been better. There was nothing available in his department so he decided to keep his eyes and ears open for something in another division. Even before the opening was "officially posted," a friend told him about the position and Lucas applied. Was his boss angry!

What Went Wrong?

Lucas seems to have done everything right except for one crucial element. He neglected to let his manager know of his intention. Company policies regarding internal moves vary considerably. In Lucas's case, his current supervisor was to be notified prior to Lucas making an application for a new position.

Successful job searches are a critical part of your career development. You always want to be thinking about and anticipating your next move either within your current organization or at another one. A mistake many people make is that they don't begin their search until they want—or worse, need—a new position.

69. Anticipate your next move.

1. *Explore your options.* Do you have specific career goals? What are your next steps? What career paths exist in your company?

What do you have to do to follow one of them? Do you need additional or new experience to move up? Will you need to change areas within your company to get the experience you need? Will you need to go to another company to get the experience that you need? Devote some time to thinking your options through and periodically reevaluate your progress.

2. *Know your company's procedures.* Many companies post openings on their website or publish a list that is available from the human resources department. Note that you may have to follow a certain protocol to interview for a different department within your company. Don't make the mistake Lucas made; find out what the proper procedure is.

3. *Stay focused.* It's easy to avoid looking. Set a number of activities, contacts, or connections that you will make each week. Make it a realistic number and work to achieve it.

4. *Be accountable to someone.* Find a coach or mentor with whom you check in periodically. Let him or her know how your search is progressing. Use your coach to brainstorm additional ideas.

5. *Schedule time for your search.* Life is hectic, but with a schedule you are more apt to find the time to look. One director I know would put his son to bed at eight o'clock and twice a week used the rest of his evening to practice interviewing.

6. *Fine-tune your résumé and cover letter.* Always keep your résumé up-to-date. If you wait until the last minute, you might forget to include an important accomplishment, and if you happen to suddenly hear about that dream job, you'll have it ready at a moment's notice. Remember, too, that your résumé

and cover letter must be perfect—no typos, no errors in grammar or spelling. It's also helpful to prepare any other materials
that you may need. Last but not least, always use good-quality
stationery; ideally your résumé and cover letter should be on
the same stationery.

If you create a blog or website to let people know about you,
make sure it looks professional. Also, remember that what you
write and put on it can help or hurt you. There was a story
recently in my local paper about people getting recruited or
fired based upon what was in their blogs.

7. *Use your network.* Let people know you are looking. You
never know where the lead will come from.

Practice, Practice, Practice: The Job Interview

Sofia was excited. She was interviewing at a prestigious firm for her very first job. Her grades were good and she had interned at a good firm in Boston, where she'd gone to school. But this was New York—the big time—and she had her hopes riding on this interview. It started out well. But then one of the partners asked the $64,000 question: Describe a time when you feel you made a good decision, and explain why. A textbook interview question, but when it came time to answer all Sofia could think of was the night she and a group of friends were out celebrating and drinking a lot and her buddy Jeff got really drunk, and she insisted he not drive and called a cab for him. She knew it was the wrong story, but she plowed on, feeling the job slip through her fingers. She was right; she didn't get the offer. She'll not use that story again.

What Went Wrong?

Good decision; wrong story. You don't want to talk about going out drinking on a job interview. As Sofia recognized, she was being asked a standard interview question—one that could be found in any number of books on interview techniques. She should have had an answer down pat to that and the myriad other interview standards that are all designed to give the interviewer a glimpse at the person you are, how you react under stress, how quick on your feet you are, and so on. It's great to illustrate such questions with what I call "the stories of your life." Prepare a bunch of them that you can call upon at a moment's notice. You can modify them to suit the occasion.

70. Be prepared for the interview.

1. *Practice.* Role-play the interview with a friend or colleague. Anticipate the tough questions and decide how to answer them. I coach professionals on how to answer interview questions, and I know that practice builds confidence.

   - *Tell me three negatives about you.* You can't ignore the question, but you want to turn the negatives into positives.

   - *What separates you from the other candidates that I will see?*

   - *Describe a situation where you were able to keep an open mind and remain nonjudgmental in spite of the circumstances.*

2. *Bring extra copies of your résumé.* You need to be prepared in case your interviewer has misplaced the one you sent, or it turns out you are interviewing with more than one person. Bring any other materials you may want to show the interviewer; for example, samples of your work if you are a writer or illustrator; designs if you're an architect; sales letters, catalogs, or brochures you may have developed, and so on.

3. *Arrive on time.* It seems obvious, I know, but not everyone remembers how important it is to be on time. If you are driving, anticipate traffic; if you take public transportation, expect the bus to be late or the train to break down. No matter how you travel, assume you will get lost.

4. *Greet the interviewer(s).* Shake hands firmly; if there is more than one person, shake each one's hand. Wait until you are offered a chair before you sit down.

BLUNDER BUSTER

In the category of how to bust someone else's blunder and to illustrate just how important being on time really is, consider this tale of woe:

A young man arrived at his interview at a financial services company ten minutes *before* his scheduled time. He thought the interview went well, and was surprised when he didn't get the job. He checked with a friend at the company and learned that although they liked him, they felt that someone who was late for an interview would not be a good employee. It turned out that the receptionist, who was extremely busy that day, hadn't notified the manager of his arrival until ten minutes after the appointment time.

The story has a happy ending. In a note to the manager, the ingenious young man explained what happened without blaming the receptionist. He was called in again and got the job.

5. *Answer questions clearly and concisely.* Do not ramble. Some interviewers are very reassuring; you may actually know your interviewer. Regardless, don't allow yourself to become too casual or too comfortable. Never forget that it's an interview, and you've got to be on your toes!

▶ **QUICK TIP:** Learn from each interview. What went right? What can you improve upon? Review the questions you were asked. How did you answer them? How will you answer them in the future?

Pachter's Pointer: Honesty *is* the best policy.

A consultant in California was hired to locate candidates for a high-level position. The screening interview for one of the candidates was held on a golf course, since the consultant knew the candidate was a good golfer and thought it would be good to get to know him outside of the office. Unfortunately, the candidate cheated when he thought no one was looking, and never got to the next interview.

6. *Mind your body language.* Your words may be saying "yes, yes," but your body may be saying, "no, go away." Keep your facial expression pleasant, look your interviewer in the eye, and avoid nervous gestures, such as wringing your hands or playing with pens or rings, which make you seem distracted.

7. *Dress appropriately.* People judge you on your appearance, so you want what you wear to work for you. This is true, regardless of the job for which you are applying.

I know the hiring manager of a local car dealership who told me about a woman who had applied to him for a job as a receptionist. She came to the interview in jeans, a shirt with her belly showing, and flip-flops. "I know a car dealership is not a big corporate environment and it's not a high-level job," he said, "but she has to meet our customers; she can't look like that!" I wholeheartedly agree.

8. *Send thank-you notes.* Write to each of the people who interviewed you. Use nice-quality, professional-looking stationery, and make certain you have made no spelling errors or mistakes.

The following story is one for the books—*Ripley's Believe It or Not*—and falls under the heading "Won't they ever learn?" but I know for a fact that it's a true story. An HR specialist let people know that the hiring manager was a stickler, and would *not* hire someone who did not write a thank-you note. Still, some candidates didn't bother to write a note. You can bet that they weren't considered for the position.

Pachter's Pointer: Use email wisely.

An emailed "thank you" is a quick, informal way to say thanks, but it does not replace the personal, thoughtful quality of a handwritten note. Yet you may find yourself in an interview situation where email may be the right choice; for example, if the hiring decision is being made that day or if all of your previous correspondence and theirs has been via email.

PART SIX

What to Say When It's Hard to Say: How to Handle Difficult Communications

Difficult and challenging conversations may make you wonder why you came to work at all that day. The fact is, at work, as in life, from time to time difficult conversations are par for the course, whether they are with coworkers, managers, customers, clients, vendors, and bosses (and myriad others).

At various times on any given day, you may find yourself contending with awkward situations, giving feedback, or coping with conflict. At such times, you want to appear both "polite and powerful," a phrase I coined to describe the behavior that people ought to display in difficult situations.

It's unfortunate but true that if you are simply polite in certain situations you can get walked on. If you are only powerful, you are often seen as (and may be) aggressive. It's the combination of the two that will make you truly successful in today's business world; as well as today's social world.

Polite and powerful behavior helps people feel good about themselves, focus on what needs to be done, maintain cordial business relationships, and accomplish their goals. Why not try it?

"Oops, I Shouldn't Have Said That!": Handling Yourself with Aplomb

Laurie was quite petite, less than five feet tall. People noticed and sometimes would comment on her size. She was self-conscious about it, and the comments drove her crazy. One day, a customer said, "Boy, you are short!" "Yes, I'm short," Laurie snapped back, "but you're rude!" The customer stormed out.

What Went Wrong?

Laurie's response was equally rude. Yes, it was uncomfortable for her when anyone, including customers, said anything about her size, but chances are the customer (and anyone else who commented) was not trying to insult her. Laurie needs to find a better way to handle this recurring awkward situation.

71. When the road gets rocky.

1. *Know your line.* What difficult situations do you encounter regularly? What do you say when they occur. If you prepare a response—a polite line or two—that you can say, you will find that you are more comfortable saying it, and others are more

comfortable hearing it. As a result, what was once awkward—even embarrassing—is much less so.

I have a broken blood vessel on my cheek. People sometimes think that it is lipstick and will call it to my attention. It's awkward for me. After all, I teach etiquette, and lipstick on your cheek is not a good thing! I needed a line.

When you create your line, don't respond with your life story—which for me would be, "I have been to plastic surgeons and they tell me they can remove it, but they can't guarantee that it won't scar, and I would rather have the mark than the scar, plus my mother said it was in a good spot, so I am keeping it." That is not my line! When someone says, "Barbara you have lipstick on your cheek," I respond, "Thank you. It's permanent!" Most chuckle or laugh, and it's over!

I coached Laurie, and, after I suggested that she come up with a line, she chose, "Thanks. It's nice of you to notice." (This was better, but it is a tad sarcastic. I suggested that she stop after "Thanks.")

2. *Head it off at the pass.* In some situations, such as mine or Laurie's, you can anticipate the difficulty and have your response ready. In other instances, you can anticipate the problem and work around it so it doesn't occur. If you know, for example, that your customer has a tendency to drink too much, plan ahead and go to a restaurant where you have to bring your own wine and bring only one bottle. If a colleague has a tendency to talk too much, let him know up front that you have time constraints when you talk to him: "Hi, Ted. I have only five minutes before my next meeting, but I wanted to check in with you about that widget order. Did it get to the customer on time?"

Don't Go There!: How Not to Have a Discussion

During a break at an off-site training conference, Lonny joined his colleagues in the break room. He knew some, but not all, of the people in the group. They were discussing the death penalty—an item that had recently received a great deal of attention in the local newspapers. When he was asked his opinion, Lonny yelled, "None of your G-D business." The other attendees avoided him for the rest of the day.

What Went Wrong?

You may not like the discussion or the opinions expressed, but yelling or becoming in any way aggressive is not the answer.

Certain discussions can quickly and easily escalate into arguments, sometimes heated ones. The old but still valid rule is *don't* discuss sex, politics, or religion at work. Your opinion may be 180 degrees different from your colleagues', or you may say something that some coworkers will find insulting, or you may offend your boss. If people with whom you work disagree with your comments, your views may subtly or not so subtly alter their opinion of you, sometimes not favorably.

In addition, you also want to avoid bad-mouthing someone, telling dirty jokes, commenting on others' sexuality, and spreading rumors. Doing any of these reflects poorly on you.

72. Five ways to avoid taboo topics.

There are, however, better ways to avoid these discussions than the one Lonny chose. Consider one of these the next time you are in a similar situation:

1. *Quickly excuse yourself.* You don't always have to say something. You can politely say, "Oh, I just remembered that I have a conference call in a few minutes and I need to get my notes. See you later." If you stay and remain silent, it may appear to others that you agree with them.

2. *Change the topic.* Simply ignore the question or comment and bring up another subject; for example, you could say, "You know what I wanted to tell you . . ." You could also say, "We're never going to agree, so let's discuss something else. What do you think about our new office opening in New York?" or "I'd rather not get into this; and anyway it's too complex an issue to discuss during a ten-minute break. Let's change the subject?"

3. *Respond with humor.* Have a standard line that you can use, like, "Oh, I never discuss that in the daylight!" (Make sure you have a smile on your face and a twinkle in your eye when you say it.) My standard line—one I use in class if a participant brings up an inappropriate topic—is: "Don't go there. Don't go there," or, "I've heard them all before. Let's move on."

4. *Answer with a question.* You can answer the question with a question, thereby putting it back on the person asking. For example, in a training session, I was once asked who I was going to vote for in the next election. I answered, "Oh, who do

you want me to vote for?" And when the person answered, I replied, "I hear he is doing well in the polls."

5. *Be assertive.* You can politely but firmly tell the person, "I'm uncomfortable discussing this subject at work. Let's get back to business."

73. Sidestepping other ticklish topics.

There are, of course, other topics that you may not wish to discuss either with a particular person or at a particular time. You may, for example, be asked a question that you don't want to answer. On those occasions, try answering without really answering.

Where in the book of life does it say you have to answer every question asked of you?

Sometimes we feel compelled to answer questions, even when we don't want to. For example, those that require sharing information you don't want to share or where a completely honest answer might hurt the person's feelings.

For instance, a man recently sent me this email asking for suggestions:

> *I was recently let go from a firm because of my communication skills. Basically I tell it like it is, always truthful, but often I seem rude. People have told me I need to be tactful. I hate it when people ask me questions, like, "How do you like my new haircut?" I am not fast on my feet coming up with something positive to say about it if it is horrid.*

Instead of going into a long story, try the following:

1. *Respond neutrally.* "It's really interesting," or "It's unusual," or "Hmmmm."

2. *Describe it.* "It's very different from the last one."

3. *Ask a question.* Instead of answering the question, ask for the questioner's opinion. "What do you think about it?"

4. *Pass the buck.* "I bet everyone loves it."

"Why Didn't You Tell Me?": Saving Someone from Embarrassment

Two colleagues, Steve and Lauren, were spending the afternoon together working on a project and visiting some customers' offices. Steve's fly was down. Lauren noticed, but did not say anything. She was embarrassed and did not know what to say. Steve called that evening—furious. He kept asking, "Why didn't you say something? I can't believe you let me walk around like that all afternoon!"

What Went Wrong?

Men's zippers and women's bra straps have caused quite a bit of trouble in the workplace. People have such a difficult time when one is down and the other is showing, yet, because they feel awkward, find all sorts of reasons to say nothing. Still, people need to be, and most want to be, told about embarrassing situations, especially those that can be so easily remedied.

74. When you've got to break the news . . .

1. *Do not use hints or try to be cute.* "Tom, go to the men's room," will only confuse Tom and can backfire. One nurse, instead of telling a physician during rounds that his fly was undone, told him the barnyard door was open. The physician, getting increasingly irritated, kept repeating, "What barn door?"

BLUNDER BUSTER

This one's easy: Be direct. Just describe the situation and say:
"Tom, your fly is undone."
"Mary, your strap is showing."

2. *A note works—sometimes.* If the person is surrounded by other people and saying something might be awkward, you may want to try a note. At a company off-site retreat, a young woman handed the speaker a note letting him know about his zipper. He zipped up and kept on talking. Back in the office, her boss, who'd noticed what she'd done, complimented her for speaking up and doing it so tactfully.

Most people want to be told if something is wrong, and thank you for it. If by some chance the person responds negatively, you don't have to crawl away. You can reply with something like, "I'm surprised by your response. I thought you would want to know."

3. *Ask someone else to do it.* If you are embarrassed because of gender issues or uncomfortable about saying something for any other reason, you may be able to get someone else to do it; but if you're the only one around, don't be a chicken, just do it.

Pachter's Pointer: Not everything needs to be said . . .

Sparing others embarrassment is not a license to give your coworkers unsolicited feedback about their appearance. You would not tell someone, "Dick, your two front teeth are missing." Dick knows his two front teeth are missing!

What You *Don't* Say Also Counts: Providing Feedback

"My boss, Sam, spends one day a month with me as I visit my customers. He drives with me from customer to customer. He is supposed to observe me and provide feedback on my calls, but he never says anything, even when I ask for his comments. He spends the whole time talking on his cell phone. I can't wait to transfer out of his area!"

What Went Wrong?

An important part of any manager's job is to give feedback to his staff and, in this case, Sam's staff member wanted to hear it. Constructive feedback helps you grow and develop, yet some managers find offering feedback very difficult. They think of feedback as criticism: something negative that puts the other person down. Yet feedback can be positive *or* negative *or* both. Giving properly constructive criticism will help a person grow, and a good manager should want his staff to grow and improve.

When managers don't say anything, nothing happens. Sam hid his inability or unwillingness to provide feedback by "doing business"; that is, by talking on his cell as they drove from customer to customer. The ploy not only didn't work, it made his employee—who may have been excellent—eager to move on.

Pachter's Pointer: To Give or Not to Give Feedback . . .

Before you provide feedback to someone, ask yourself if you are the right person to give feedback.

- *If you are the boss,* it is *your responsibility* to give feedback to your employees. If you are not, you could be giving unsolicited advice, which can not only be risky, but inappropriate.

- *If you are not the boss, think twice.* Before jumping in, you can ask your colleague if he or she is open to feedback. Some people are, others are not. You can say something like, "I heard some comments about your presentation, would you like me to share them with you?"

75. How to Provide Feedback—Positively.

1. *Be specific.* Instead of saying "I believe you could do better," tell the person exactly what he was doing and suggest ways to do it better. Instead of saying "Your presentation slides were awful," say, "The slides were difficult for people to read because the font size was too small. Use 32-point type next time; that way even people in the back of the room will be able to read them." If you can, arrange for or let the person know about specific training or coaching that may be available.

2. *Mention the good, too.* Make sure you don't overwhelm employees or colleagues (or friends) with criticism and that you comment on the things they do right! Don't make something up; there is usually some positive comment you can make.

3. *Make sure you are understood.* Ask a question like, "Do you agree?" "So, the next step is . . . ," and check with the person to make sure that he or she really understands.

4. *Follow up.* Check in with the person periodically. When the person makes improvement, acknowledge it.

 Pachter's Pointer: When you are on the receiving end . . .

Ask yourself:

- *Who is giving the feedback?* If the person is an expert, the feedback is a gift and you should seriously think about what the person is saying and how to implement their ideas. If the person is a jerk, simply listen, say "Thank you," and, if the person is off base, forget about it.

  If, however, the person giving the feedback is your boss, pay attention to what is said. You may want to ask for further explanation. You can respectfully disagree and explain why, but remember rank has its privileges and unless it's unethical, you usually do what your boss wants you to do.

- *Do the comments sound familiar?* One comment—never heard again before or after—may say more about the person making the comment than it does about you. If there is a pattern to the comments you receive, chances are there is some truth to them.

When the Going Gets Rough: Responding Positively to Negative Comments

Serena was always juggling something. One day it was her kids' school schedules, on another she had four projects due, and on still another it was the last-minute details of the sales conference. Some days, like today, it all caught up with her. Her boss was about to meet with an important client and she hadn't given him the latest figures. "If you had your act together, this wouldn't have happened!" he sputtered as he ran out the door.

What Went Wrong?

Serena has too much on her plate. Some of it is in her control; some of it isn't. Regardless of the reason, the worst part about being told you did something wrong is that it usually takes you by surprise, which throws you off balance. The important thing is not to react in a way you will later regret. Though it may feel good to say, "Well, what do you know, you idiot?" that's not going to build your credibility or accomplish anything, and, if you say it to your boss, it might cost you your job.

But it is important to act. You don't want to be thinking, "I should have said . . ." When you're prepared, it's easier to retain your composure and not become defensive. Build your credibility and other people's confidence in you by following these guidelines:

76. Five ways to be graceful under fire.

1. *Agree with the comment.* A good defense is the best offense. Use the phrase "You're right." They are very powerful words. You simply agree with what the person said. "You're right. And it won't happen again." This usually stops the conversation cold. There is nothing else to be said.

    You can also agree and provide additional information that turns the comment around. For example, you might say, "You're right. We did spend a lot of money because it was important to get this information out to our customers very quickly."

    In Serena's case, she might have said (but only if it was true), "You're right. I should have had this information, but the accounting department is not releasing any information until this afternoon due to some computer glitch."

2. *Ask for clarification.* Ask questions or make comments to get more information: "Why are you saying that?" "Help me to understand what you mean by . . ." "Tell me more about your concerns." "Are you saying it was . . . ?" Probing provides you with more information, makes you less likely to appear wounded by the attack, and buys you some time to calm down and collect your thoughts.

3. *Acknowledge what you have heard.* First acknowledge what was said: "I understand your frustration," or, "I hear what you are saying." Then use the word *and* to provide clarifying information. As mentioned in Part Three, don't use *but*, use *and*. *But* negates what comes before it. A defusing statement such as, "There may be some truth to that, *and* we are looking at the numbers," or "That's interesting, *and* you may not realize

that we've also been looking at those numbers," can let the person know that you have heard what was said.

4. *Respectfully disagree.* Be polite but firm. You can say, "I disagree, and here's why . . ."

5. *Postpone the discussion.* If the statement was made in public, it sometimes is best to talk to the person privately. Say something like, "You obviously have strong feelings. Let's get together after the meeting so we can discuss this issue in more depth." You may also want to postpone the conversation, if you are caught off guard or feeling very emotional about what was said. A good way to do this is by saying, "I want to talk with you about this, and need to give it some thought. Let's meet tomorrow?"

CONFLICT, CALAMITIES, AND OTHER CATASTROPHES

Conflict Self-Assessment

Your own awareness of your confrontational style is important. Do you have a tendency to avoid conflict, become aggressive, or to handle conflict well? Take this self-assessment and find out:

Rate the degree to which you agree or disagree with the following statements:

0—*Strongly disagree*

1—*Somewhat disagree*

2—*Somewhat agree*

3—*Strongly agree*

Put your answer in the unshaded box.

When interacting with others:

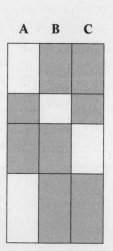

	A	B	C

1. I ignore other people's behavior even if it is bothering me.

2. I can't help it, I yell when I'm upset.

3. I tell other people about their behavior when it creates a problem for me.

4. If I have a problem with a friend, I will stop calling him or her until he or she gets the hint that I'm upset.

When interacting with others:

	A	B	C

5. I usually express myself to others in an honest, direct, and polite manner.

6. I tell other people about someone's behavior and its effect on me without talking about it directly with that person.

7. It is important that I always win or get my way.

8. I express my anger to another person without verbally attacking or blaming the other person.

9. I have hit walls or thrown things when upset.

	A	B	C

Total the number in each column:

This self-assessment is designed to raise your awareness of your confrontational style. Many things can influence your score. Some people have one style at home and one at work. Some people see themselves one way but others see them differently. Some people are unaware of their behavior and have a difficult time answering the questions.

Your highest number is your dominant style; your next highest number is your next dominant style. If you have two numbers that are the same or close, you may be going back and forth between the styles.

Your lowest number is your least dominant style. You can learn from your low numbers.

If all your numbers are low, you are either exceptionally easygoing or in deep denial; if all your numbers are high, you can be out there—doing it all.

Nonconfronter: If your total for column **A** is 6 or higher, you believe that you can have difficulty with conflict and often avoid confronting others.

Aggressive confronter: If **B** is 6 or higher, you believe that you can have difficulty with conflict and often confront others in an aggressive, negative manner.

Polite and Powerful: If **C** is 6 or higher, you believe that you can confront people, and usually handle conflict well.

"Keep It Outside": An Office Is Not a Boxing Ring

Two competing pharmaceutical sales representatives met at a doctor's office. They started arguing, which escalated to yelling, about who had the next appointment. The physician, who had to break up the argument, told both to never come back again.

What Went Wrong?

Screaming and yelling in business situations is simply never acceptable. Even if you are right, when you engage in such unprofessional and negative behavior, you look bad.

Work out your differences politely and powerfully.

77. Grow up!

In business, you should not:

1. *Get into fistfights.* Nothing more needs to be said about this one, I hope!

2. *Stop talking to the other person.* You don't need to be best friends, but you have to work together. One boss would not talk to one of his employees. He communicated with him through his administrative assistant!

3. *Assume and/or act without all the information.* We can be very quick to say things and, when we don't know all the facts,

we frequently regret them. It's not so easy to repair the damage and it can negatively affect your career advancement.

4. *Stir things up by saying foolish things.* Your goal should be to make the situation better, not worse. Why say things, such as:

   "I've been yelled at by better."

   "I would be bothered by that if I gave a damn about what you thought."

   Instead, why not try:

   "Screaming at me will not help us (or help me/help you) solve the problem. It will only make us both look bad (or unproductive)."

5. *Cast blame.* Avoid blaming "you" statements. If you say, *"You are not carrying your weight,"* it will be viewed as an attack. Use "I" statements, instead. *"I need more help,"* is more likely to receive a positive response.

 Pachter's Pointer: Look at your own behavior.

Many times we help cause or contribute to the problem and don't realize it. I have presented hundreds of seminars to thousands of people and no one in any of my classes has ever been the cause of the problem. I believe them!

It's How You Say (or Don't Say) It That Counts

Olivia, a sales rep, went to her customer's office at the appointed time for a lunch meeting only to be told that her customer was gone for the day, and that the appointment wasn't on his calendar. Olivia exploded at the receptionist. The head of the department, her customer's boss, heard the ruckus and told Olivia never to come back.

Kevin, a direct report to Don, goes over Don's head to his boss to alert him of problems. Don says nothing to Kevin and Kevin keeps on telling tales.

What Went Wrong?

Many conflicts aren't dealt with properly. People either explode as Olivia did or they don't say anything, as Kevin did, and nothing changes.

In both cases, the results can be costly. There is, however, a middle ground. You can be "polite and powerful" in situations that are otherwise ripe for conflict.

78. Seven ways to be politely powerful.

1. *Pick your conflict.* You can't fight them all. You can't win them all. And beyond all that, who cares! (Some would say "pick your battles," but that's too negative.) Choose the conflicts that matter most and ones that will have an effect on your career or that you have some influence over. If the issue isn't important, why not let it go? You'll be less stressed if you do.

2. *Use "Pachter's Jerk Test."* We are very quick to make negative assumptions about others. Although sometimes it may feel that way, most people are not jerks. Perhaps, more important, most people are not out to get us. At the same time, many people become preoccupied and don't realize how their behavior affects others. If you approach someone thinking that person is a jerk, it is very easy to explode. Say to yourself, *Maybe the person's a jerk, maybe not, I'll find out.* You are more likely to stay polite and powerful.

 Pachter's Pointer: Nobody's perfect: "I accept your quirks because you accept mine."

> Somebody's late, somebody's early; your boss gives you last-minute deadlines that aren't really necessary or could have been avoided by planning ahead; a coworker borrows stuff and doesn't return it: all of these situations are ripe for conflict, but in some cases the best response is no response. You have little quirks of your own; if you ignore theirs, they are more likely to ignore yours and your office relationships will be more pleasant.

3. *Set the stage.* If you do confront a situation, as Kevin should have, there are a number of things that will help the confrontation go more smoothly.

- *Keep it private.* It's embarrassing to the other person if you confront in public.

- *Do it in person.* Email and the telephone have their place in our business lives, but they tend not to work when you must confront another person. Often a person becomes more upset that you wouldn't discuss the issue face-to-face than he would have been about the issue itself.

- *Do it when you are calm.* If you are not calm, it's usually best to postpone; otherwise, it's too easy to explode.

- *Do it at the right time.* Choose a time that's good for the other person. If she's walking out the door for a meeting, that's not the time to confront her!

▶ **QUICK TIP:** If your colleague is anything like my husband, make sure he has been fed!

4. *Discuss one issue at a time.* You don't want to confuse things or overwhelm the other person. What's more, you are less likely to get sidetracked if you stick to just one issue.

5. *Prepare and practice.* You are less likely to explode or wimp out if you do. Your wording should be specific, direct, polite, and nonaccusatory. (See WAC'em below)

6. *Pay attention to your nonverbal body signals.* Have you ever heard yourself say, "But I didn't mean it that way!" Chances are your words said one thing but your body language or voice sent a different message.

Pachter's Pointer: WAC'em . . . with your words.

WAC'em is an acronym I created to provide an alternative to not confronting a person or confronting a person aggressively. It's not an either/or proposition: You don't have to avoid people or attack them; you can choose to WAC'em with your words—calmly, directly, specifically, and in a nonaccusatory manner. You are moving into the Polite and Powerful (P&P) middle.

Don't Confront	P&P	Confront Aggressively

Don't attack 'em, WAC'em. Here's how:

- **W** is for **WHAT.** What's *really* bothering you? Use polite wording to define the problem. You need to be specific about what the person has done and you may have to explain the effect the person's behavior has on you.

- **A** is for **ASK**. What do you want to ask the other person to do or change? What's going to solve the problem? Again, you need to be specific and ask for what is possible.

- **C** is for **CHECK IN**. What is the other person's reaction? You need to check in and find out.

How to create your WAC

- *Write* down what you want to say. It can help clarify the problem and eliminate the negativity from your language.

- *Practice—aloud, if possible.* Hear how the words sound. If they sound harsh to you, they will sound harsh to the listener. Change them.

7. *Apply WAC'em technique.* Here's an example of a WAC that worked:

The principal of the high school had dropped into Miriam's tenth-grade history class. It was a rough day and the kids were not being responsive. About halfway into the class, the principal interrupted and, in essence, took over teaching the class. Miriam was fuming, but said nothing. After the class, she scheduled an appointment and confronted the principal. She was very proud of herself and told me her WAC really worked well. Here's what she said:

WHAT: "You may not realize that when you started teaching my class today, you, in effect, took over the class. This really affects the way the students will look at me in the future and makes it harder for me to gain their respect and cooperation."

ASK: "In the future, I would appreciate it if you would let me continue the class and discuss any problems with me after class is over."

CHECK-IN: "Okay?"

A consultant/friend of mine said he tried WACing his waitress when he was out to lunch with a client. As he tells it, he did not like the waitress's greeting. He is a jokester so did he really do this? I don't know and he wouldn't say. Either way it's fun, and a good example of a WAC.

Waitress: How're you guys doing today?

WHAT: "We're fine, but when you call us 'you guys' we are offended by it."

ASK: "We'd prefer just plain 'you.'"

CHECK-IN: "Could you accommodate us with that?"

Waitress: "Sure. Are you *kids* ready to order?"

79. WAC'em Exercise.

Practice your new skills and create your WAC'em words for these situations. They are real-life conflicts that have been told to me in various seminars.

1. *The late worker.* Your coworker routinely makes appointments and he or she is either late or doesn't show. It really messes up your schedule. You decide to confront this person.

2. *The weekend traveler.* Your boss assumes that you are available to travel over weekends for meetings because you are single and have fewer priorities than your colleagues who are married, either with or without children. You would like to

have some time at home, too. After much soul-searching, you decide to confront the boss.

3. *The sexy dresser.* Your colleague sometimes does not dress professionally and that bothers you. You have heard negative comments from your customers about how she looks. You believe that she is not exemplifying the company's standard. You decide to confront.

4. *The voicemail monster.* Your coworker usually takes four to five days to respond to your voicemail messages. The other members in your group are very good at returning messages in a timely manner. You don't want to keep calling this person—it wastes your time! You decide to confront.

5. *The friendly employee.* You have a new employee. He is very friendly and an excellent worker, yet his attempts at humor aren't working. He has used inappropriate sexual innuendo in conversations and jokes about other nationalities. You need to stop this before it goes any further. You decide to confront.

One last thing: Don't WAC the big one tomorrow! Start slowly on little conflicts. Over time you will increase your expertise and confidence. (Additional information on "Don't Attack 'em, WAC'em" can be found in my book *The Power of Positive Confrontation*.)

CONCLUSION

The Next Step

A final reminder . . .

A man in my class was returning home from a business trip and was at the airport waiting in line to talk to the ticket agent. The couple in front of him was having problems with their tickets; they were yelling and extremely rude to the ticket agent, who kept her cool and took care of their problems. After they left, the man heard the agent at the next counter say, "Boy they were really being nasty to you!" The agent replied, "That's okay. They are going to London; their luggage is going to Bulgaria!"

There are lots of reasons to exhibit good manners, least of which is that you don't want your luggage going to Bulgaria!

It's my hope that the blunders you've read about here have made etiquette easy and fun to read about, and, more important, that they will help you remember how you do and do not want to behave throughout your business career. It always pleases me when someone tells me—years after attending a seminar—that something similar happened and they remembered a particular story and knew exactly how to handle it.

It's not always easy to change habits built over a lifetime, so as you begin to try out new behaviors, remind yourself that you can't change everything at once. Pick a few things and practice your new skills until you feel comfortable with them. After a while, you'll find they become second nature and you won't really have to think consciously about them anymore. Then pick a few more. Gradually over time, you will notice a difference in how you are interacting with people and how they are responding to you.

Remember, too, that we all make mistakes, some of them quite inadvertent; as was the case of a manager, who said to a new colleague, "I love the color of your contacts." She responded, "I am not wearing contacts." *Ouch!* The manager quickly recovered, and said, "Your eye color is so beautiful it's nice to know that it's not man-made!"

You won't be able to retrieve all of the blunders all of the time; however, by applying the things you've learned here, we're hoping the slip-ups will be few and far between. If you do put your foot in your mouth, keep the following Blunder Busters in mind:

1. Turn a faux pas into a compliment, if you can.

2. Anticipate and prepare.

3. Know your line.

4. Ignore it and just continue.

5. Admit it.

6. Make it right or take action.

7. Use humor, if you can and if it really is funny. Remember to laugh along.

8. Try again.

And, of course, when there is no possibility for recovery, and your foot is planted in your mouth, learn from it and don't do it again!

ACKNOWLEDGMENTS

I would like to thank all the seminar participants who willingly shared their stories and their blunders with me. They gave of themselves and I am truly grateful. We laughed and learned together. I would also like to thank Christel Winkler, my editor, for her wisdom and flexibility; Ellen Coleman, for her gift of words; and Joyce Hoff, for her support. Last but not least, my husband, Martin; my son, Jacob; and the rest of my growing family. Their encouragement sustains me.

—Barbara Pachter

INDEX

ABOUT THE AUTHORS

Barbara Pachter is a highly respected speaker, trainer, and coach specializing in business etiquette, business communications, and assertiveness issues. She has delivered more than 1,600 seminars throughout the world including the first-ever seminar for businesswomen in Kuwait. Her client list features major corporations and organizations worldwide, including DaimlerChrysler, Genentech, Citigroup, Pfizer Inc., NASA, Merck & Co., and Microsoft.

Pachter is the author of *When the Little Things Count . . . And They Always Count* and *The Power of Positive Confrontation*. She is also the coauthor of several books including the groundbreaking *Complete Business Etiquette Handbook* and *The Jerk with the Cell Phone: A Survival Guide for the Rest of Us.*

She has appeared on *20/20* and CNN, and has been featured in numerous publications including the *New York Times, Harvard Business Review,* and *Washington Post.*

Barbara Pachter can be reached at:

Pachter & Associates
P.O. Box 3680
Cherry Hill, NJ 08034
856-751-6141
pachter@ix.netcom.com
www.pachter.com

258   *About the Authors*

Ellen Schneid Coleman, a former publishing executive for Prentice Hall Press, edited Barbara's first book, *The Complete Etiquette Handbook.* She now heads Ellen Schneid Coleman Literary Services, which offers complete editorial services to authors and publishers. She has written, edited, or packaged numerous books including *The Scholarship Book* and the eight-book On the Road series devoted to personal finance.